WELCOME TO HISTORIC SCOTLAND

Scotland's built heritage is a precious resource, which Historic Scotland protects for present and future generations. This guide contains details of the many historic properties across Scotland, which are cared for by Historic Scotland. From prehistoric dwellings to stone circles, abbeys to cathedrals, castles to palaces — there is more than 5000 years of Scottish history waiting to be discovered and enjoyed.

A free brochure containing opening times and admission charges can be obtained from our staffed properties, our headquarters at Longmore House, Salisbury Place, Edinburgh EH9 1SH, telephone 0131 668 8800 or at many other outlets around Scotland.

Guidebooks relating to the properties plus a range of publications on historic themes can be purchased from Longmore House, telelephone 0131 668 8752, or at many of our properties. The proceeds from admissions and purchases support Historic Scotland in its conservation and presentation work. Wherever possible the merchandise is sourced in Scotland with an emphasis on supporting local craft industries.

During the summer, a programme of battle re-enactments, drama, music and other events brings the vivid impact of living history to many sites. Ask for a brochure for more details or telephone 0131 668 8830.

D0271236

ABOUT HISTORIC SCOTLAND

Historic Scotland safeguards the nation's built heritage on behalf of the Scottish Ministers and promotes its understanding and enjoyment. We maintain over 300 properties in the care of the Scottish Ministers, and operate the largest number of visitor attractions in Scotland.

Scotland has a wealth of ancient monuments and historic buildings and structures. Historic Scotland and its team of archaeologists, historians, conservators, architects, technical staff, draughtsmen and managers care about them all.

Legal protection is given to the more important ancient monuments and historic buildings, to guard them against damaging changes or demolition. There are more than 52,000 protected ancient monuments and historic buildings, including prehistoric burial tombs, standing stones, castles, churches, great houses, thatched cottages, lighthouses, bridges and industrial buildings.

Advice and grants are provided to help with the specialist care which historic structures need.

Historic Scotland advises and helps everyone involved in giving a future to Scotland's built heritage. Our conservation centre carefully restores paintings and stonework. As part of the task of safeguarding the built heritage, research is carried out into better ways of caring for Scotland's monuments and buildings and managing them for the future.

Historic Scotland's education service operates a free educational visits scheme to the properties in care and provides teaching resources and activities linked to the 5-14 Curriculum. The Education Service can be contacted on 0131 668 8732.

FREE ENTRY TO ALL HISTORIC SCOTLAND PROPERTIES

Join the Friends of Historic Scotland and get free entry to all Historic Scotland properties. With over 5000 years of Scotland's history to explore, membership offers fantastic value for money. By joining you will also be making an important contribution to the preservation of Scotland's built heritage for future generations.

Membership benefits include:

• Free entry to all Historic Scotland properties, including Edinburgh and Stirling Castles.

• 20% retail discount in Historic Scotland shops, including books, clothing and gifts.

• Free quarterly magazine keeping you informed with features on history and heritage, conservation projects and places to visit.

• Free or discounted entry to over 300 Historic Scotland events from battle re-enactments to medieval cookery displays.

• Half price entry to over 500 heritage attractions in England, Wales and the Isle of Man in your first year of membership with free entry in your second and subsequent years.

English Heritage, tel: 01793 414 910. www.english-heritage.co.uk

CADW:Heritage in Wales, tel: 029 2050 0200. www.cadw.wales.gov.uk

Manx Heritage, tel: 01624 648 000. www.gov.im/mnh

• The opportunity to take part in members' activities from guided tours and lectures to ceilidhs and cruises.

Membership is available on an annual or life basis, with a range of categories to choose from. You can join at any staffed Historic Scotland property or by calling 0131 668 8999 with your credit/debit card details or to request an information pack.

5000 YEARS OF SCOTTISH HISTORY

PREHISTORY

The prehistoric monuments in Historic Scotland's care include some of the finest in Europe, with the Northern and Western Isles being particularly rich.

In recognition of their outstanding value, several of the Orkney sites dating back to 3000-2000 BC, have been inscribed by UNESCO as The Heart of Neolithic Orkney World Heritage Site. These are Skara Brae, northern Europe's best preserved Neolithic stone-built village, Maes Howe burial mound, an exceptionally early architectural masterpiece; the Stones of Stenness, a unique and early expression of the ritual customs of Neolithic peoples; and the Ring of Brogar, the finest truly circular late Neolithic or early Bronze Age stone ring.

Shetland has the intriguing Neolithic complex at Staneydale and the amazingly well preserved Mousa Broch, as well as Jarlshof, where one can take a walk through the past from prehistory into history. On Lewis, the mysterious stone circle, avenue and alignments at Calanais, dramatically set against mountain and sea, are also outstanding.

On the mainland, there are rich seams of prehistory to be explored in the Highlands of Scotland, most notably the Grey Cairns of Camster in Caithness and the enchanting Clava Cairns near Culloden; along the Kilmartin Glen, Argyll, which has some of the best examples of Bronze Age rock art anywhere in Britain; across Galloway, with two well-preserved chambered tombs at Cairn Holy; and in Grampian, with its concentration of recumbent stone circles including Easter Aquhorthies and Loanhead of Daviot.

Other highly significant sites are at Cairnpapple Hill (Lothian), a great ceremonial place throughout prehistory; Edin's Hall Broch (Borders), one of the most southerly brochs set within a large hill fort; and the Brown and White Caterthuns (Angus & City of Dundee), two great hill forts, one of earth and one of stone. In the Angus & City of Dundee area, there survive several souterrains, or underground storage chambers, such as that at Ardestie.

THE ROMANS

The land now known as Scotland lay on the north west frontier of the Roman Empire. Roman armies invaded Scotland several times, sometimes defeating the northern tribes but never incorporating them into their empire. The nature of the contact between Rome and her northern neighbours was thus primarily military, and the surviving monuments reflect this. Nearly all the monuments only survive today as earthworks, but they are a

remarkable group and of international importance.

Each time the Roman army set up camp, it protected itself by constructing a rampart and ditch, and parts of two such camps may be seen at Black Hill, Ardoch (Perthshire). When the empire ceased expanding, its borders were protected by frontiers. Parts of one such line survives in Perthshire and is represented by the watchtowers at Muir o' Fauld and Ardunie, which appear to date to the 1st century AD.

Shortly after their construction the Romans withdrew to the Tyne-Solway line, where they built Hadrian's Wall in the 120s. That Wall, in turn, was succeeded in the 140s by the new frontier line – the Antonine Wall – constructed across central Scotland from sea to sea. This frontier, which only lasted about 20 years, can still be traced intermittently today. Behind the Wall lay forts and fortlets that housed the troops charged with the duties of defending the province and controlling its inhabitants in the border regions. These military installations were linked by roads, such as Dere Street at Soutra beside the A68 (Borders).

THE EARLY MEDIEVAL PERIOD

For the visitor wishing to see tangible evidence of the early medieval period in Scotland (cAD400 – 1000), a real challenge waits. The craggy rock of Dunadd in Argyll was an important stronghold of the Dalriadic kings of Argyll from the late 5th century, and the footprint and other carvings on its summit may be linked to the inauguration ceremony of these predecessors of the kings of Scotland. On the eastern slope of Doon Hill, by Dunbar, can be seen the outline of the foundations of a British lord's feasting hall and that of his Anglian successor.

Sites associated with religious life are more prominent. Whithorn, St Ninian's 'cradle' of Christianity in Scotland', has an important collection of sculpture including the earliest Christian memorial in Scotland. In the west, there are enchanting remains of early Christian monasteries on Iona, at St Blane's (Bute) and on the islands of Eileach an Naoimh and Eilean Mor (Argyll). To complement the monasteries, Argyll has a marvellous heritage of Christian sculpture, including the high cross at Kildalton on Islay.

Little Pictish settlement survives in Historic Scotland's care, except at Gurness and Brough of Birsay, but ancient Pictland is a treasure house of sculpture. Fine collections of their enigmatic symbol stones can be seen at Meigle and St Vigeans (Angus & City of Dundee). Also significant are the stones at Aberlemno, the internationally significant St Andrews Sarcophagus and the great cross-slab known as Sueno's Stone at Forres.

For Viking enthusiasts, Orkney and Shetland are both must-see destinations. Settlement sites at Jarlshof and the Brough of Birsay are complemented by other sites with Norse connections; Maes Howe with its fascinating, witty and occasionally lewd runic graffiti; the 12th-century round church at Orphir; the 12th-century church of St Magnus on Egilsay with its magnificent round tower and one of Scotland's earliest stone castles, Cubbie Row's on the Island of Wyre.

THE MIDDLE AGES AND LATER

Scotland is as rich in monuments of the Middle Ages as any European country. For the castle explorer, mighty fortresses, middling strongholds and minor lairds' houses can be found from Unst (Shetland) to Hermitage (Borders). There are the

great royal castles such as Stirling and
Edinburgh in Scotland's earliest historic
burghs, powerful baronial houses such as
Tantallon (Edinburgh & Lothians) and
Bothwell (Greater Glasgow & Clyde
Valley), and modest towers such as
Smailholm (Borders). Of particular
interest is the group of early stone castles
in Argyll, including the MacDougall
stronghold of Dunstaffnage.

Religious life in medieval Scotland is
reflected in the great cathedrals of
Glasgow, St Andrews and Dunkeld,
imposing monasteries such as those in the
Border Abbey, Dumfries and Galloway and
on Iona, which has recently come into the
care of Historic Scotland, where there also
survives a very rare medieval nunnery,
parish churches such as St Clement's at
Rodel, Harris, and collegiate kirks such as
Seton (Edinburgh & Lothians) and
Lincluden (Dumfries & Galloway). Their
tombs and heraldry bear witness to
Scotland's great families.

The Reformation of 1560 saw the demise
of the great medieval religious buildings,
and the invention of the gun effectively put
paid to castles as military strongholds.

Imposing Craignethan Castle (Greater
Glasgow & Clyde Valley) was one of the
last great medieval castles to be built in
Scotland. However, Jacobite disaffection in
the late seventeenth and eighteenth
centuries saw the erection of purpose-built
fortresses by the Government, including
Ruthven Barracks (Highlands), built after
the rising of 1715, and Fort George
(Highlands), the mighty garrison fortress
built in the aftermath of Culloden.

The modern era is represented by a small
but important collection of industrial
monuments, including Bonawe Furnace
(Argyll), the most complete charcoal-
fuelled ironworks surviving in Britain, and
the working New Abbey Corn Mill
(Dumfries & Galloway). The Blackhouse
complex at Arnol, Lewis, provides a rare
and fascinating insight into domestic life in
a crofting township, while Sunnybrae
Cottage, the earliest house in Pitlochry
(Perthshire), is a type of domestic house
once so common in the Highlands and
now very rare.

HOW TO USE THIS GUIDE

Areas

Scotland has been divided into 14 tourist board areas ranging from the Scottish Borders in the south to Shetland in the north, see the map on the inside cover. Within each area, sites are listed alphabetically and there is also a full alphabetical index of all sites on pages 77-80.

Maps

Maps at the start of each area listing help you to locate sites. A full-size Historic Scotland map is available from shops at sites or from our headquarters at Longmore House.

Friends

Friends of Historic Scotland enjoy free entry to all properties, excluding Holyrood Abbey, which is within the grounds of the Palace of Holyroodhouse, in Edinburgh.

Safety

Visiting some sites can involve a fair amount of walking over uneven ground. Sensible footwear is recommended. Watch out for wet grass on sloping banks and wet wooden footbridges.

Opening Times and Admission Prices

The majority of Historic Scotland's properties are free and open to the public at any time. Some are operated under key keeping arrangements. Properties that are staffed and have an admission price follow the opening times shown below unless directed otherwise in the text.

Admission prices are for the period 7 January 2002 to 6 January 2003. Children under the age of 16 must be accompanied by an adult. Most of the staffed properties offer free quiz sheets for children to use during their visit. Please ask on arrival.

Summer (April to September) Properties with an admission charge are open seven days a week, Monday to Sunday from 9.30am to 6.30pm. Some properties have special opening times shown against their entry in this guide.

Winter (October to March) Some of our properties with an admission charge close. The rest are open Monday to Saturday from 9.30am to 4.30pm and from 2.00pm to 4.30pm on Sunday – except where special opening times are shown in this guide. Extended opening times may also apply during the "Autumn Gold" months of October and November – please telephone for details. All of our properties where admission is charged close on Christmas Day and Boxing Day. Please telephone to check New Year opening.

With so much to see please leave plenty of time to visit before the property closes for the evening. We sell the last ticket 30 minutes before the property closes and 45 minutes before closing at the larger properties of Edinburgh, Stirling and Urquhart Castles and Fort George.

Some of the smaller properties may close for a short period over lunch. Please telephone to check.

To check the property you wish to visit is open, telephone the number shown against the entry or call our visitor information service on 0131 668 8800.

Public Transport

By Air

The majority of internal flights are operated by British Regional Airlines, tel: 0845 7733377, www.britishairways.com

By Rail

National Rail Enquiries, tel: 08457 484950. For advance credit/debit card bookings contact Scotrail telesales, tel: 08457 550033.

By Coach

The main operator in Scotland is Scottish Citylink Coaches, tel: 08705 505050, www.citylink.co.uk

The Postbus carries fare paying passengers in rural areas where there is no other form of transport. Contact the Royal Mail for more information and timetables, tel: 0131 228 7407.

By Ferry

The West

Caledonian MacBrayne, tel: 01475 650100. For reservations tel: 08705 650000, www.calmac.co.uk

Western Ferries, operators of services across the Clyde between McInroy's Point (near Gourock) and Hunters Quay (near Dunoon), tel: 01369 704452, www.western-ferries.co.uk

Serco Denim operates the service between Islay and Jura on behalf of the Argyll and Bute Council, tel/fax: 01496 840681.

Orkney and Shetland

P&O Ferries, tel: 01224 572615, www.poscottishferries.co.uk

John O' Groats Ferry, tel: 01995 611353 www.jogferry.co.uk

Orkney Ferries Ltd, tel: 01856 872044.

Orkney travel information available on www.visitorkney.com

Timetables available from Shetland Islands Tourism, tel: 01595 693434, www.shetland-tourism.co.uk

National Timetable

For all bus, rail and coach enquiries call the National Public Transport Timetable on 0870 6082608

World Heritage Sites

Properties with World Heritage recognition feature a UNESCO logo.

Quality Assurance

Visitor facilities at Historic Scotland staffed properties are inspected by VisitScotland.

Visitors with Disabilities

The wheelchair symbol indicates that visitors in wheelchairs can enjoy a reasonable amount of the property. Where there are toilets suitable for wheelchair users, this is indicated by a WC next to the symbol. Other special facilities for people with a disability are indicated in the site descriptions.

A free leaflet outlining facilities and access at staffed properties for people with disabilities is available, free of charge, from Historic Scotland headquarters or from staffed properties. A large print version of Historic Scotland's brochure promoting the 70 staffed properties is also available from Longmore House and the properties.

A large print text version of this guide can also be requested from Longmore House.

Guidebooks

Guidebooks, postcards and quality souvenirs are available at most staffed properties. A publications catalogue is available by telephoning 0131 668 8752.

Dogs

Dogs on leads are permitted at some but not all properties. Please telephone the property you wish to visit in advance to check.

Symbols

The symbols underneath each site description indicate the range of facilities available and whether there is an entrance fee.

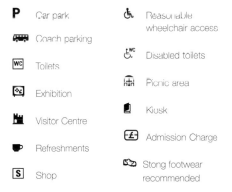

P Car park	♿ Reasonable wheelchair access
🚌 Coach parking	
WC Toilets	♿^{WC} Disabled toilets
Exhibition	⛱ Picnic area
Visitor Centre	Kiosk
Refreshments	Admission Charge
S Shop	Stong footwear recommended

11.

12.

8.

SCOTTISH BORDERS

1. CROSS KIRK, PEEBLES

In Cross Road, Peebles on the A703.
NT 250 407.

The nave and west tower of a Trinitarian Friary, founded in the late 13th century with foundations of the domestic buildings.

&

2. DERE STREET ROMAN ROAD, SOUTRA

Beside Soutra Aisle, just off the A68 on the B6368. 73 NT 452 580.

A good stretch of the Roman road running from Corbridge, beside Hadrian's Wall, to Cramond on the Firth of Forth. Beside the road are quarry pits from which the gravel for building the road was taken,

3. DRYBURGH ABBEY

7M SE of Melrose, near St Boswells. Turn left on to the B6356 from the B6404. 74 NT 591 316.

Both beautifully situated and of intrinsic quality, the ruins of the Premonstratensian abbey at Dryburgh are remarkably complete. Much of the work is of the 12th and 13th century. Sir Walter Scott and Field Marshall Earl Haig are buried in the abbey. Tel: 01835 822381.

★★★★ Grading
Admission: Adult £2.80
Child £1.00 Reduced £2.00

3.

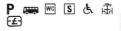

4. EDIN'S HALL BROCH

On the NE slope of Cockburn Law, about 4.5M from Grantshouse, 1m walk from the A6112 Duns road, then a footpath for 2M. 67 NT 772 603.

One of the few Iron Age brochs in lowland Scotland. Unusually large, it sits in a fort defended by ramparts and ditches, partially overlain by a settlement of the Romano-British period.

P

5. EDROM CHURCH

In Edrom, 3.5M NE of Duns just off the A6105. 67 NT 827 558.

The richly carved Romanesque doorway of the old parish church of Edrom, in the kirkyard.

P

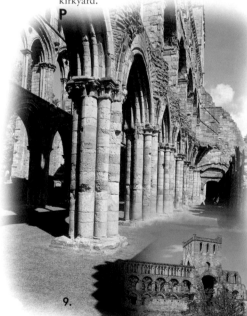

9.

6. FOULDEN TITHE BARN

In Foulden 4M SE of Chirnside on the A6105. 67 NT 931 558.

A two-storey barn used for storing payments made in grain to the parish church. View exterior only.

7. GREENKNOWE TOWER

0.5M W of Gordon on the A6105 Earlston road. 74 NT 639 428.

A handsome tower house on an L plan, built in 1581 and still retaining its iron gate or yett.

8. HERMITAGE CASTLE

In Liddesdale, 5.5M NE of Newcastleton, off the B6399. 74 NY 494 961.

A vast and eerie ruin of the 14th and 15th centuries, associated with the de Soulis, the Douglases and Mary Queen of Scots. Partly restored in the 19th century. Nearby is the 14th-century Hermitage Chapel. Open summer only. Tel: 01387 376222.

★★★ Grading.
Admission: Adult £2.00 Child 75p
Reduced £1.50

9. JEDBURGH ABBEY

In Jedburgh on the A68. NT 650 204.

One of the border abbeys, founded by David I around 1138 for Augustinian canons. The church is built in the Romanesque and early Gothic styles and is remarkably complete. Remains of the cloister buildings have been uncovered and finds from the excavations, including the 12th-century 'Jedburgh comb', are on display. Tel: 01835 863925.

★★★★★ Grading.
Admission: Adult £3.30 Child £1.20
Reduced £2.50

10. KELSO ABBEY

In Kelso. NT 728 338.

The west end of the great abbey church of the Tironensians, brought to Kelso in 1128 by David I. Even in its fragmentary state, this is a superb piece of architecture.

&

11. MELROSE ABBEY

In Melrose off the A7 or A68. NT 548 341.

Probably the most famous ruin in Scotland, the abbey was founded by David I in 1136 for the Cistercian Order, it was largely destroyed by Richard II's English army in 1385. The surviving remains of the church are largely of the early 15th century, and are of an elegance unsurpassed in Scotland. Objects found during excavation are displayed in the Commendator's House. Audio guide available.
Tel: 01896 822562.

★★★★ Grading.
Admission: Adult £3.30 Child £1.20
Reduced £2.50

P 🚐 [WC] [⊠] [🏰] [☕] [S] [♿] [🚻] [£]

12. SMAILHOLM TOWER

Nr Smailholm village, 6M W of Kelso on the A6089. Then on to the B6937, turning on to the B6404. 74 NT 638 346.

Sited high on a rocky outcrop, Smailholm is a small rectangular tower set within a stone barmkin wall. Inside the tower is a model of this Pringle residence and a charming collection of costume figures and tapestries relating to Sir Walter Scott's *Minstrelsy of the Scottish Borders*. It was the sight of Smailholm that fired Walter Scott's imagination when, as a young boy, he was brought up by his grandparents at the nearby farm of Sandyknowe. Open all summer and weekends in winter.
Tel: 01573 460365.

★★★★ Grading.
Admission: Adult £2.00 Child 75p
Reduced £1.50

P 🚐 [⊠] [£] [👣]

10.

11.

27.

23.

26.

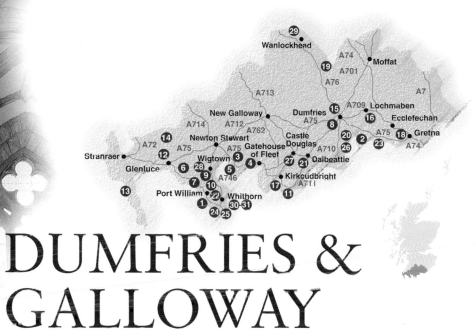

DUMFRIES & GALLOWAY

1. BARSALLOCH FORT

On the edge of a promontory above
Barsalloch Point, 0.75M W of Monreith on
the A747. 83 NX 347 412.

An Iron Age promontory fort, defended by
a deep u-shaped ditch. A steep climb.

P

2. CAERLAVEROCK CASTLE

8M SE of Dumfries on the B725.
84 NY 025 656.

This is one of the finest castles in Scotland.
Its most remarkable features are the twin-
towered gatehouse and the Nithsdale
Lodging, a splendid Renaissance range
dating from 1638. Children's adventure
park and replica siege engines in front of
castle and nature trail to the old castle,
recently excavated and currently being laid
out for visitors. Café and new exhibition
on siege warfare. Tel: 01387 770244.

Admission: Adult £2.80 Child £1.00
Reduced £2.00. ★★★★★ Grading

P 🚌 WC 📷 🏰 ♿ S ♿ ♿ 🚻 💷

3. CAIRN HOLY CHAMBERED CAIRNS

6.5M SE of Creetown, on the A75.
83 NX 518 540.

Two remarkably complete Neolithic burial
cairns, of a type characteristic of Galloway,
situated on a hill with fine views over
Wigtown Bay.

P

2.

4. CARDONESS CASTLE

1M SW of Gatehouse of Fleet on the A75. 83 NX 590 552.

The well-preserved ruin of a tower house of 15th-century date, the ancient home of the McCullochs. The architectural details inside the tower are of a high quality and there are good views over Fleet Bay from the battlements. New scale model and exhibition on the history of the castle. Open all summer and at weekends in winter. Tel: 01557 814427.

Admission: Adult £2.20 Child 75p Reduced £1.60.

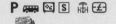

4.

5. CARSLUITH CASTLE

3.5M S of Creetown on the A75. 83 NX 494 541.

The delightful and well-preserved ruin of a tower house of 16th-century date. The 18th-century ranges of outhouses are still in use by the farmer, reminding the visitor that such houses were originally linked to outbuildings. One of its owners was the last abbot of Sweetheart Abbey. The site is open during the standard opening times published in this guide.

6. CHAPEL FINIAN

5M NW of Port William on the A747. 82 NX 278 489.

The foundation remains of a small chapel in an enclosure, built in the Irish style, probably as a chapel for pilgrims on their way to Whithorn, having landed at the nearby shore.

7. DRUCHTAG MOTTE

At Mochrum village on the A747. NX 349 466.

A fine example of a motte castle, in a part of Scotland where this type of early timber castle proliferated in the 12th and 13th centuries. A very steep climb.

8. DRUMCOLTRAN TOWER

7M NE of Dalbeattie, among farm buildings off the A711. 84 NX 869 682.

A well-preserved tower of mid16th-century date simply planned and built, sitting within a busy modern farmyard. The site is open during the standard opening times published in this guide.

P

9. DRUMTRODDAN CUP AND RING MARKED ROCKS

2M NE of Port William on the B7085. 73 NX 362 447.

Three groups of well-defined cup and ring marks on bedrock probably carved in the Bronze Age. Part of an important prehistoric landscape.

10. DRUMTRODDAN STANDING STONES

0.25M S of the cup and ring marked stones on the B7085. 83 X 364 443.

An alignment of three stones, one of which has fallen. Together with 9, part of an important prehistoric landscape.

11. DUNDRENNAN ABBEY

6.5M SE of Kirkcudbright on the A711.
84 NX 749 475.

The beautiful ruins lie in a peaceful setting, of a Cistercian abbey founded in 1142 by David I. The east end of the church and the chapter house are of exceptional architectural quality. Mary Queen of Scots spent her last night on Scottish soil here in May 1568. Open all summer and at weekends in winter. Tel: 01557 500262.

★★★ Grading.
Admission: Adult £1.80 Child 75p
Reduced £1.30

P 🚌 ♿ ◾ £

12. GLENLUCE ABBEY

2M NW of Glenluce village off the A75.
82 NX 185 586.

A Cistercian abbey founded around 1192. The remains, including a handsome early 16th-century chapter house, are set in a lovely tranquil valley. An exhibition of objects found at the abbey is on display at the site. Open all summer and at weekends in winter. Tel: 01581 300541.

Commended
Admission: Adult £1.80 Child 75p
Reduced £1.30

P 🚌 ☒ ☕ Ⓢ ♿ £

12.

13. KIRKMADRINE EARLY CHRISTIAN STONES

In the Rhinns of Galloway, 2M SW of Sandhead on the A716. 82 NX 080 483.

Three of the earliest Christian memorial stones in Britain, dating from the 5th or early 6th century, displayed in the porch of a former chapel.

14. LAGGANGAIRN STANDING STONES

At New Luce on the Southern Upland Way about 5M from Balmurrie Farm by foot. From New Luce take the minor road past the church to Balmurrie Farm.
82 NX 222 716.

Two stones carved with early Christian crosses. Difficult access signposted through Forestry Commission land on the Southern Upland Way.

🚲

15. LINCLUDEN COLLEGIATE CHURCH

On the western outskirts of Dumfries in Abbey Lane on the A76. NX 966 779.

The remains of a collegiate church and the accommodation for its canons founded in 1389 by Archibald the Grim, 3rd Earl of Douglas (see Threave Castle) on the site of an earlier nunnery. The splendid chancel was probably added by his son Archibald, the 4th Earl, and houses the exquisite monumental tomb of his wife, Princess Margaret, daughter of Robert III. The site is open during the standard opening times published in this guide.

16. LOCHMABEN CASTLE

On the shore of Lochmaben Loch 1.5M from Lochmaben on the B7020.
78 NY 088 811.

The much reduced remains of a royal castle originally built by the English in the 14th century but extensively rebuilt during the reign of James IV (1488-1513). Largely dismantled after its capture by James VI in 1588. View exterior only. The extensive remains of earthworks, including a rectangular 'peel' (timber palisaded enclosure) built by Edward I of England, are visible around the masonry castle.

P

17. MACLELLAN'S CASTLE

In Kirkcudbright on the A711.
NX 682 510.

A castellated town house, complete except for its roof, built by the then provost of Kirkcudbright, Thomas MacLellan of Bombie, in the 1570s but probably never finished. Open summer only.
Tel: 01557 331856.

★★★★ Grading.
Admission: Adult £2.00 Child 75p
Reduced £1.50

⬚S⬚ ⬚£⬚

21.

18. MERKLAND CROSS

At Woodhouse Farm 1M N of Kirkpatrick Fleming on the B7076. 85 NY 250 721.

A fine carved wayside cross, of 15th-century date.

19. MORTON CASTLE

Majestically situated on a promontory overlooking Morton Loch. Take the second turning on the right, 1.5M E of Carronbridge off the A702.
78 NX 891 992.

A fine late 13th-century hall house, a stronghold of the Douglases.

20. NEW ABBEY CORN MILL

In New Abbey village, 7M S of Dumfries on the A710. NX 962 662.

A carefully renovated water-powered mill, in working order, and demonstrated regularly to visitors in the summer months. A video, The Millers Tale, is on show inside the mill. Mill demonstration 12.00 noon and 3.00pm in summer. Closed Thursday afternoon and Friday in winter.
Tel: 01387 850260.

★★★★ Grading.
Admission: Adult £2.80 Child £1.00
Reduced £2.00
Joint ticket with Sweetheart Abbey available: Adult £3.50 Child £1.20
Reduced £2.50

⬚▣⬚ ⬚▥⬚ ⬚S⬚ ⬚▦⬚ ⬚£⬚

21. ORCHARDTON TOWER

6M SE of Castle Douglas on the A711.
84 NX 817 551.

A charming little tower house of mid-15th-century date. It is, uniquely, circular in plan. The site is open during the standard opening times published in this guide.

P

22. RISPAIN CAMP

1M W of Whithorn, behind Rispain Farm on the A746. 83 NX 429 399.

A rectangular settlement defended by a bank and ditch. It dates from the 1st or 2nd century AD.

23. RUTHWELL CROSS

At Ruthwell 8.5M SE of Dumfries, sited within the parish church on the B724.
NX 100 682.

This Anglian Cross, sculptured in high relief, dates from the end of the 7th century AD and is considered one of the major monuments of early medieval Europe. Access can be arranged during published opening times by contacting the keykeeper, tel: 01387 870249.

P

24. ST NINIAN'S CAVE

Physgill, on the coast 4M SW of Whithorn on the A747. 83 NX 421 359.

Traditionally associated with St Ninian. Early crosses found here are housed at Whithorn Museum, but weathered crosses carved on the walls of the cave are still visible.

P 🚌 🐾

25. ST NINIAN'S CHAPEL

At Isle of Whithorn on the A747. NX 807 598.

Restored ruins of a 13th-century chapel, probably used by pilgrims on their way to Whithorn.

P 🚌

26. SWEETHEART ABBEY

In New Abbey village, 7M S of Dumfries on the A710. NX 965 622.

The splendid ruin of a late 13th-century and early 14th-century Cistercian abbey founded by Devorgilla, Lady of Galloway, in memory of her husband John Balliol. Apart from the abbey church, the principal feature is the well-preserved wall, enclosing the abbey precinct. Closed Thursday afternoons and Fridays in winter. Tel: 01387 850397.

★★★ Grading.
Admission: Adult £1.80 Child 75p Reduced £1.30. Joint ticket with New Abbey Corn Mill available: Adult £3.50 Child £1.20 Reduced £2.50

P 🚌 ♿ 🛍 £

27. THREAVE CASTLE

3M W of Castle Douglas on the A75. 84 NX 739 623.

A massive tower built in the late 14th century by Archibald the Grim, Lord of Galloway. Round its base is an artillery fortification built before 1455, when James II besieged the castle. It is on an island, approached by boat. Approximately 0.25M, but flat, walk to property. Open summer only. Tel: 0831 168512.

★★★ Grading.
Admission: Adult £2.20 Child 75p Reduced £1.60. Ferry included in admission price.

P 🚌 WC 🚻 🛍 £

28. TORHOUSE STONE CIRCLE

4M W of Wigtown on the B733. 83 NX 382 565.

A Bronze Age stone circle consisting of 19 boulders. This type of stone circle is most commonly found in north-east Scotland and is therefore unusual for this area.

29. WANLOCKHEAD BEAM ENGINE

In Wanlockhead village off the A76.

An early 19th-century wooden water-balance pump for draining a lead mine, with the track of a horse engine beside it. Nearby is the privately operated museum of Scottish lead mining.

30 AND 31. WHITHORN PRIORY AND MUSEUM AND THE MONREITH CROSS

In Whithorn on the A746. NX 444 402.

One of the earliest Christian sites. Whithorn was traditionally founded by Ninian in the 5th/6th century. Later a priory for Premonstratensian canons was built in the 12th century and became the cathedral church of Galloway. In the museum is a fine collection of early Christian carvings, including the Latinus stone, the earliest Christian memorial in Scotland, and the Monreith Cross, the finest of the Whithorn school of crosses. The Monreith cross was probably carved here in the 10th or 11th century. Joint ticket with the Whithorn Trust. Open Easter to October 10.30am to 5.00pm. Tel: 01988 500508.

(Historic Scotland Friends retail discount not eligible).
Admission: Please telephone for details.

 ♿ £

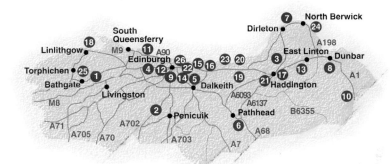

EDINBURGH & LOTHIANS

1. CAIRNPAPPLE HILL

3M N of Bathgate, 1.25M from Torphichen, 4M from Linlithgow off the A706. 65 NS 987 717.

One of the most important prehistoric monuments on the mainland of Scotland, Cairnpapple was used as a burial and ceremonial site from about 3000 to 1400 BC. Good views of east central Scotland may be had from the hill. Open summer only. Tel: 01506 634622.

★★★★ Grading.
Admission: Adult £1.80 Child 50p Reduced £1.30.

P ☒ Ⓢ ☲ ☜

2. CASTLELAW HILL FORT

On Castle Knowe, about 1M NW of Glencorse or 2.5M SW from Lothianburn Junction on the City Bypass, off the A702. 66 NT 229 638.

An Iron Age hill fort with a souterrain built in one of the ditches.

P ☒ ☜

3. CHESTERS HILL FORT

1M S of Drem off the B1377. 66 NT 507 782.

One of the best-preserved examples in Scotland of an Iron Age fort defended by an elaborate system of ramparts and ditches.

P ☜

4. CORSTORPHINE DOVECOT

In Dovecot Road off Saughton Road N leading to and from Corstorphine High Street, Edinburgh. NT 200 725.

A large circular 'beehive' dovecot in a good state of preservation with nesting boxes complete.

5. CRAIGMILLAR CASTLE

2.5M SE of Edinburgh, off the A68. NT 283 705.

Built round an L-plan tower house of the early 15th century, Craigmillar was much expanded in the 15th and 16th centuries. It is a handsome ruin, including a range of private rooms linked to the hall of the old tower. Closed Thursday afternoons and Fridays in winter. Tel: 0131 661 4445.

Admission: Adult £2.20 Child 75p
Reduced £1.60.
★★★ Grading.
Green Tourism Bronze Award

P 🚌 WC 🖼 🏛 🍵 S ♿wc £

6. CRICHTON CASTLE

2.5M SSW of Pathhead off the A68.
66 NT 380 611.

A large and sophisticated castle, of which the most spectacular part is the range erected by the Earl of Bothwell between 1581 and 1591. This has a facade of faceted stonework in an Italian Renaissance style. Open summer only. Tel: 01875 320017.

★★★ Grading.
Admission: Adult £2.00 Child 75p
Reduced £1.50.

P 🚌 📖 £ 👞

7. DIRLETON CASTLE AND GARDEN

In the village of Dirleton, 3M W of North Berwick on the A198. NT 516 839.

The oldest part of this romantic castle dates from the 13th century. It was partly rebuilt in the 14th century and modified in the 16th century. Beside the castle lie the gardens, first recorded in the 16th century. Existing gardens include an early-20th-century 'Arts and Crafts' garden and a restored Victorian garden. The *Guinness Book of Records* has authenticated the herbaceous border as the world's longest. Tel: 01620 850330.

★★★★ Grading.
Admission: Adult £2.80 Child £1.00
Reduced £2.00.

P 🚌 🖼 S ♿ ♿wc £

8. DOONHILL HOMESTEAD

2M S of Dunbar, off the A1.
67 NT 686 755.

The site marked out in the grass, of a wooden hall of a 6th-century British chief, and of an Anglian chief's hall, which superseded it in the 7th century, revealed by aerial photography followed by excavation in the 1960s. A rare record of the Anglian occupation of southeast Scotland.

P

9. DUPPLIN CROSS

In the National Museum of Scotland, Chambers Street, Edinburgh.

The magnificent 9th-century Dupplin Cross was recently moved from its site at Forteviot in Perthshire to help preserve the splendid carvings that decorate every face of the cross. Presently on loan to to the National Museum of Scotland, the cross is due to be housed in St Serf's Church, Dunning near Forteviot early in 2002.

10. DUNGLASS COLLEGIATE CHURCH

1M NW of Cockburnspath off the A1. 67 NT 766 718.

Founded in 1450 for a college of canons by Sir Alexander Hume. A handsome cross-shaped building with vaulted nave, choir and transepts, all with stone slab roofs.

P

11. EAGLE ROCK, CRAMOND

On the shore of the Forth about 0.25M W of Cramond off the A90. To visit the Rock visitors must cross the River Almond by a small boat. 66 NT 184 774.

A much-defaced carving on natural rock said to represent an eagle.

👞

7.

12. EDINBURGH CASTLE

In the centre of Edinburgh. NT 252 734.

This most famous of Scottish castles has a complex building history. The oldest part, St Margaret's Chapel, dates from the 12th century; the Great Hall was erected by James IV around 1510; the Half Moon Battery by the Regent Morton in the late 16th century; and the Scottish National War Memorial after the First World War. The castle houses the Honours (Crown Jewels) of Scotland, the Stone of Destiny, the famous 15th-century gun Mons Meg, the One o' Clock Gun and the National War Museum of Scotland. In addition to guided tours provided by the castle stewards, there is an audio guide tour available in six languages. The Crown Jewel shop in the Royal Apartments offers exclusive lines of specially designed jewellery. A courtesy vehicle (provided by the Bank of Scotland) can take visitors with a disability to the top of the castle. Ramps and a lift give access to the Crown Jewels, Stone of Destiny and associated exhibition; and ramps provide access to the war memorial. For those with impaired vision, there is a free Braille guide and hands-on models of the Crown Jewels with Braille texts. Parking is restricted from June to October for the Edinburgh Military Tattoo. Tel: 0131 225 9846.

Open all year seven days a week. April to September 9.30am to 6.00pm. October to March 9.30am to 5.00pm. Last ticket sold 15 minutes before closing. Closed Christmas Day and Boxing Day. ★★★★★ Grading. Admission: Adult £8.00 Child £2.00 Reduced £6.00.

13. HAILES CASTLE

1.5M SW of East Linton of the A1. 67 NT 574 757.

A beautifully sited ruin incorporating a fortified manor of 13th-century date, extended in the 14th and 15th centuries. There are two vaulted pit-prisons.

14 AND 15. HOLYROOD ABBEY AND ABBEY STRAND

Holyrood Abbey: At the foot of the Canongate, Edinburgh, in the grounds of the Palace of Holyroodhouse. Abbey Strand: At the foot of the Royal Mile, at the gates of the Palace of Holyroodhouse. NT 269 739.

The ruined nave of the 12th and 13th century abbey church, built for Augustinian canons. Abbey and palace administered by the Lord Chamberlain. There is no free entry for Friends of Historic Scotland to Holyrood Abbey. The three-storey building on Abbey Strand has its origins in the late 15th or early 16th century. It was partly rebuilt in 1544 and was heavily restored in 1916. The buildings to the east began as an extension to the west tenement in the mid 16th century. Abbey Strand currently houses a Historic Scotland bookshop.

16. HOLYROOD PARK

In Edinburgh, E of Holyrood Palace and Abbey. NT 2773.

Holyrood Park is a unique historic landscape in the heart of the city, whose dramatic crags and hills give Edinburgh its distinctive skyline. Within the Park is a wealth of history and archaeology spanning thousands of years. Arthur's Seat is one of four hill forts, dating from around 2000 years ago. East of Dunsapie Crag is a prehistoric farmstead of scooped circular huts. St Anthony's Well, a stone bowl and massive boulder, lies on a path up to the gaunt ruin of St Anthony's

Chapel, which stands on a spur overlooking the Forth. Downhill is St Margaret's Well, one of seven holy wells in the Park. The remains of medieval and later rig-and-furrow cultivation can be seen in several places. A Royal Park probably since the 12th century, Holyrood Park was enclosed by a stone-built boundary wall in 1541. As well as its rich cultural heritage, the Park offers walks, solace, wildlife, volcanic geology and unparalleled vistas of the city from its many vantage points. There is an exhibition in Holyrood Lodge Information Centre and the Holyrood Park Ranger Service also provides visitor services. Parking on Broad Pavement by the Palace. Tel: 0131 556 1761.

P 👟

17. LAUDERDALE AISLE, ST MARY'S CHURCH

In Haddington on the A1. NT 518 736.

The former sacristy of the great 15th-century parish church, with a splendid monument of early 17th-century date, in marble, with alabaster effigies.

18. LINLITHGOW PALACE

In Linlithgow off the M9. Exit M9 at Junction 3 northbound or Junction 4 southbound. NT 002 773.

The magnificent ruin of a great Royal Palace set in its own park and beside Linlithgow Loch. A favoured residence of the Stewart kings and queens from James I (1406-37) onward. Building work commissioned by James I, III, IV, V and VI can be seen. The great hall and chapel are particularly fine. James V (1512) and Mary Queen of Scots (1542) were both born here. Tel: 01506 842896.

★★★★ Grading.
Admission: Adult £2.80 Child £1.00 Reduced £2.00.

P ⅏ 🐾 Ⓢ 🚻 ♿

19. ORMISTON MARKET CROSS

In the village of Ormiston, 2M S of Tranent off the A1. NT 414 692.

Symbol of the right of the inhabitants to hold a market, this is a fine free-standing 15th-century cross on a modern base.

20. PRESTON MARKET CROSS

0.5M S of Prestonpans off the Coast Road or 0.5M NE of the B1361 near the railway station. 66 NT 391 740.

The only surviving example of a market cross of its type on its original site. A beautiful piece of early 17th-century design, with a cylindrical base surmounted by a cross-shaft headed by a unicorn. View from the outside.

21. ST MARTIN'S KIRK, HADDINGTON

On the eastern outskirts of Haddington off the A1. NT 521 739.

The ruined nave of a once splendid Romanesque church, altered in the 13th century. Associated with the Cistercian nunnery St Mary's, founded in Haddington before 1159.

22. ST TRIDUANA'S CHAPEL, RESTALRIG COLLEGIATE CHURCH

Off Restalrig Road South, on the east side of Edinburgh. NT 283 743.

The lower part of a chapel built by James III, housing the shrine of St Triduana, a Pictish saint. The hexagonal vaulted chamber is unique. Access can be arranged Monday to Friday from 9.00am to 5.00pm by contacting St Margaret's Parish Church, Restalrig, tel: 0131 554 7400.

18.

23. SETON COLLEGIATE CHURCH

1M SE of Cockenzie off the A198, the main Edinburgh to North Berwick road or 1M W of Longniddry on the A198.
66 NT 418 751.

The chancel and apse of this lovely building are of 15th-century date, and the transepts and steeple were added by the widow of the Lord Seton who was killed at Flodden in 1513. Open summer only.
Tel: 01875 813334.

★★★ Grading.
Admission: Adult £1.50 Child 50p
Reduced £1.10.

P 🚌 🅿 📗 💷

24. TANTALLON CASTLE

3M E of North Berwick off the A198.
67 NT 595 850.

A remarkable fortification built by the Red Douglasses, on a promontory, with earthwork defences and a massive 14th-century curtain wall with towers. During the 16th century the castle was strengthened to resist artillery, with a forework to protect the central tower. The castle had a stormy history owing to its strategic position. Interpretative displays include a replica gun. Closed Thursday afternoons and Fridays in winter.
Tel: 01620 892727.

★★★★ Grading.
Admission: Adult £2.80 Child £1.00
Reduced £2.00.

P 🚌 wc 🅿 S ♿ 💷

25. TORPHICHEN PRECEPTORY

In Torphichen village. 1M on the B792 from A706.

The tower and transepts of a church built by the Knights Hospitaller of the Order of St John of Jerusalem in the 13th century, much altered. Open summer on Saturdays (11.00am-5.00pm) and on Sundays and bank holidays (2.00pm-5.00pm).
Tel: 01506 653733.
Admission: Adult £1.50 Child 50p
Reduced £1.00.

P 🚌 wc 🅿 📗 💷

26. TRINITY HOUSE

99 Kirkgate, Leith, Edinburgh, EH6 6BJ

Trinity House is the home of the Incorporation of Shipowners and Shipmasters. An organisation dating back to the 14th century. Successive generations of Masters and members of Trinity House have been closely involved in the history and maritime development of Leith. Thomas Brown designed the present Trinity House in 1816 on the site of the medieval mariner's hospital. This fine Georgian building contains a unique collection of maritime artefacts.
Open all year. Guided tours only. Contact Steward in advance to arrange booking. No disabled access. Good public transport links. Parking not guaranteed.
Tel: 0131 554 3289 Fax: 0131 554 1273
Admission: Adults £2.50 Children £1.00 Reduced £1.90. 10% discount for group bookings.

24.

A914
Newburgh
A91
Cupar ⑨⑩ ⑪ St Andrews
⑧⑫
⑭
A916
Glenrothes A917
③
A915
⑦
Kirkcaldy
M90
A907
Dunfermline
A985 ④⑤
②
⑬ ①
⑥

KINGDOM OF FIFE

1. ABERDOUR CASTLE AND GARDEN

In Aberdour 5M E of the Forth Bridges on the A921. A short walk from the railway station. NT 192 854.

A 13th-century fortified residence, extended in the 15th, 16th and 17th centuries with splendid residential accommodation and a terraced garden and bowling green. There is a fine circular dovecot. Closed Thursday afternoons and Fridays in winter. Tel: 01383 860519

★★★★ Grading
Admission: Adult £2.20 Child 75p
Reduced £1.60.

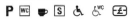

2. CULROSS ABBEY

At the head of the village of Culross off the A985. Access by foot from nearby parking on the shores of the Forth. NS 989 862.

The remains of a Cistercian monastery founded in 1217. The eastern parts of the Abbey Church are the present parish church. There are ruins of the nave, cellars and domestic buildings.

3. DOGTON STONE

In a field at Dogton farmhouse, 1.5M ENE of Cardenden railway station off the B922. Not signposted. 58 NT 236 968.

Once a splendid free-standing cross, probably of 9th-century date, all that now remains is a much weathered fragment, best appreciated when appropriate lighting conditions highlight the surviving decoration.

📖

4 AND 5. DUNFERMLINE PALACE AND ABBEY

In Dunfermline just off the A907. Road signing to nearby car park. NT 090 873.

The remains of a great Benedictine abbey founded by Queen Margaret in the 11th century. The foundations of her church are under the present superb nave, built in the 12th century in the Romanesque style. Robert the Bruce was buried in the choir, now the site of the present parish church (closed during the winter). Substantial parts of the Abbey buildings remain, including the vast refectory. Next to the Abbey is the ruin of the Royal Palace built from the guesthouse of the monastery and altered in the 16th century for James VI and his Queen. This was the birthplace of Charles I, the last monarch born in Scotland. Closed Thursday afternoons and Fridays in winter. Tel: 01383 739026.

★★★★ Grading.
Admission: Adult £2.20 Child 75p
Reduced £1.60

6.

6. INCHCOLM ABBEY

On Inchcolm in the Firth of Forth. Reached by public ferry from South Queensferry (30 mins). NT 189 826.

The best-preserved group of monastic buildings in Scotland, founded around 1123, includes a 13th-century octagonal chapter house. Ferries from South Queensferry (Tel: 0131 331 4857) and North Queensferry. Open summer only. Tel: 01383 823332.

Admission: Adult £2.80 Child £1.00
Reduced £2.00.
★★★ Grading.

7. RAVENSCRAIG CASTLE

On the eastern outskirts of Kirkcaldy, off the A955 Dysart Road. NT 290 924.

One of the earliest artillery forts in Scotland, it was begun for James II in 1460. It consists of two round towers linked by a cross range. The west tower was the residence of James II's widow, Queen Mary of Gueldres.

P

8. ST ANDREWS CASTLE

In St Andrews on the A91, on the sea front just off North Street. NO 512 169.

The ruins of the castle of the Archbishops of St Andrews, dating in part from the 13th century. Notable features include a 'bottle-dungeon' and mine and counter-mine tunnelled during the siege that followed the murder of Cardinal Beaton in 1546. These siege works are the finest of their kind in Europe. A fascinating exhibition in the visitor centre brings the history of the castle and cathedral to life. Sunday morning open 9.30am all year. Tel: 01334 477196.

Admission: Joint ticket with the Cathedral available: Adult £4.00 Child £1.25 Reduced £3.00.
★★★★ Grading.

8.

9. ST ANDREWS CATHEDRAL AND ST RULE'S TOWER

In St Andrews on the A91, on the sea front at the head of North Street. NO 513 166.

The remains of the largest cathedral in Scotland, and of the associated domestic ranges of the priory. The precinct walls are particularly well preserved. The Cathedral Museum houses an outstanding collection of early and later medieval sculpture and other relics found on the site, including the magnificent St Andrews Sarcophagus of Pictish date. St Rule's Tower, in the precinct, is part of the first church of the Augustinian canons at St Andrews built in the early 12th century. There are splendid views from the top. Sunday morning open 9.30am all year. Tel. 01334 472563.

Admission: Joint ticket with the Castle available: Adult £4.00 Child £1.25 Reduced £3.00. ★★★★ Grading.

9.

10. ST ANDREWS: BLACKFRIARS CHAPEL

In South Street. NO 507 165.

A vaulted side apse survives of this church of Dominican friars, which was built in about 1516.

11. ST ANDREWS: ST MARY'S CHURCH, KIRKHEUGH.

On the sea front beside St Andrews Cathedral. NO 515 166.

The scanty foundations of a small cruciform church on the edge of the cliff behind the cathedral. It was the earliest collegiate church in Scotland. Destroyed at the Reformation.

12. ST ANDREWS: WEST PORT

In South Street. NO 506 165.

One of the few surviving city gates in Scotland, built in 1589 and renovated in 1843. View exterior only

13. ST BRIDGET'S KIRK, DALGETY

On the shores of the Forth, 2M SW of Aberdour off the A921. 66 NT 169 838.

The shell of a medieval church, much altered in the 17th century for Protestant worship. On the west end is a burial vault with laird's loft above, built for the Earl of Dunfermline.

14. SCOTSTARVIT TOWER

3M S of Cupar off the A916. 59 NO 370 112.

Probably built in the 15th century, and remodelled between 1550 and 1579. Renowned as the home of Sir John Scot, author of *Scot of Scotstarvit's Staggering State of the Scots Statesmen*. It is a particularly handsome and well-built tower. Keys are available from Hill of Tarvit House. Open summer only.

P

11.

13.

14.

7.

GREATER GLASGOW & CLYDE VALLEY

ANTONINE WALL MONUMENTS (Nos 1 - 5)

The Antonine Wall was Rome's north-west frontier, it ran for 37 miles from Bo'ness to Old Kirkpatrick. It consisted of a turf rampart fronted by a ditch; with forts about every two miles, and a road running for the entire length of the frontier. The Wall was built in the 140s AD and occupied for about 20 years. See also Antonine Wall entries in Argyll, The Isles, Loch Lomond, Stirling & Trossachs section.

1. ANTONINE WALL: BEARSDEN BATH-HOUSE

On Roman Road, Bearsden, Glasgow. Signed from Bearsden Cross on A810. Approximately 600 metres down Roman Road. NS 546 720.

The well-preserved remains of a bath-house and latrine, built in the 2nd century AD to serve a small fort.

&. 🥾

2. ANTONINE WALL: BAR HILL FORT

0.5M E of Twechar, signposted from village. Access from B8023 Kirkintilloch to Kilsyth Road. 64 NS 706 759-714 762.

The highest fort on the line of the Wall, containing the foundations of the headquarters building and bath-house. To the east sits a small Iron Age fort. The Wall ditch runs past both. This is the best site to appreciate the strategic significance of the Wall and enjoy the superb views over the Kelvin Valley.

🥾

3. ANTONINE WALL: CROY HILL

Between Croy and Dullatur. Access from B802. 64 NS 725 762-739 769.

The fort here is not visible, but the Wall ditch survives well and there are two beacon platforms. Here the Romans had to cut through solid rock to create the ditch.

🥾

4. ANTONINE WALL: DULLATUR

0.5M E of Dullatur off the A803. Access along farm road.
64 NS 751 772-756 773.

A well preserved section of ditch.

5. ANTONINE WALL: CASTLECARY TO WESTERWOOD (GARNHALL DISTRICT)

West of Castlecary off the B816. Access from minor road.
64 NS 769 777-783 782.

A well preserved section of ditch.

6. BAROCHAN CROSS

In Paisley Abbey, in the centre of Paisley.
NS 485 639.

A fine free-standing early medieval cross that formerly stood in Houston parish, west of Paisley.

7. BIGGAR GASWORKS MUSEUM

In Biggar. Located in Gas Works Road off A702 Edinburgh to Abington road.
72 NT 038 376.

Typical of a small town coal-gas works, Biggar's is the only one surviving in Scotland. The oldest part of the works dates from 1839. Managed by the Biggar Museum Trust. Open daily 2.00pm-5.00pm June to September. Tel: 01899 221050.

P WC ⊠ £⊟

8. BOTHWELL CASTLE

At Uddingston off the B7071. Exit M74 at Junction 5 north and southbound or from the A8 take the A75 to Uddingston.
NS 688 593.

The largest and finest 13th-century stone castle in Scotland, much fought over during the Wars of Independence. Part of the original circular keep survives, but most of the castle dates from the 14th and 15th centuries. In a beautiful setting overlooking the Clyde. Closed Thursday afternoons and Fridays in winter.
Tel: 01698 816894.

★★★★ Grading.
Admission: Adult £2.00 Child 75p
Reduced £1.50.

P 🚌 WC ⊠ S £⊟

8.

9. CADZOW CASTLE

In the grounds of Chatelherault Country Park, Hamilton. Exit M74 at Junction 6. NS 735 537.

Constructed between 1500 and 1550, Cadzow Castle was known as the castle in the woods of Hamilton. Sir James Hamilton of Finnart built it for his half brother, the second Earl of Arran. At present, only the exterior of the castle can be viewed.

10. COULTER MOTTE

1.5M SW of Biggar. On A73 Biggar to Lanark road. 72 NT 018 362.

A good example of a Norman castle mound, which would have been surmounted by a palisade and timber tower.

11. CRAIGNETHAN CASTLE

5.5M WNW of Lanark off the A72. Exit M74 at Junction 10 northbound or Junction 7 southbound. 71 NS 815 463.

In a picturesque setting overlooking the River Nethan. The oldest part is a tower house built by Sir James Hamilton of Finnart in the 16th century. The castle is particularly noted for its artillery fortifications. Open summer only. Tel: 01555 860364.

★★★ Grading.
Admission: Adult £2.20 Child 75p
Reduced £1.60.

P ⓦ ⒨ 🚻 Ⓢ £

12. CROOKSTON CASTLE

Off Brockburn Road, Pollok, SW of Glasgow city centre. Exit M8 at Junction 26. NS 525 627.

The altered ruin of an unusual 15th-century castle, consisting of a central tower with four square corner towers, set within 12th-century earthworks. Affords excellent views of south-west Glasgow. The site is open during the standard opening times published in this guide.

13. GLASGOW CATHEDRAL

In central Glasgow. Exit M8 at Junction 15. NS 603 656.

The only Scottish mainland medieval cathedral to have survived the Reformation complete (apart from its western towers). Built during the 13th to 15th centuries over the supposed site of the tomb of St Kentigern. Notable features in this splendid building are the elaborately vaulted crypt, which includes an introductory display and collection of carved stones, the stone screen of the early 15th century and the unfinished Blackadder Aisle. Not open to visitors on Sunday morning in summer.
Tel: 0141 552 6891.

Ⓢ

14. NEWARK CASTLE

In Port Glasgow on the A8. Turn right at Newark roundabout.

The oldest part of the castle is a tower built soon after 1478, with a gatehouse. The connecting range was added in 1597-99 by the wicked Patrick Maxwell, in a most elegant style. Open summer only.
Tel: 01475 741858.
★★★ Grading.
Admission: Adult £2.20 Child 75p
Reduced £1.60.

P 🚌 ⓦ 🦽 Ⓢ £

15. ST BRIDE'S CHURCH, DOUGLAS

In Douglas. Access from the A70 Lanark to Cumnock road, follow signs. 72 NS 835 309.

The choir and south side of the nave of a late 14th-century parish church. The choir contains three canopied monuments to the Douglas family, including the tomb of Good Sir James who famously carried Bruce's heart on Crusade. Access during published opening hours can be arranged by contacting the key keeper, tel: 01555 851657.

31

29.

50.

55.

45.

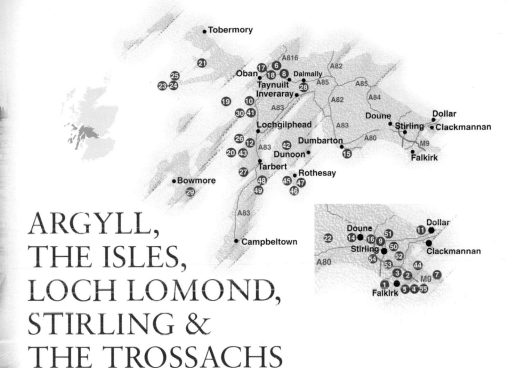

ARGYLL, THE ISLES, LOCH LOMOND, STIRLING & THE TROSSACHS

ANTONINE WALL MONUMENTS (Nos 1-5)

See also entries in Greater Glasgow & Clyde Valley section.

1. ANTONINE WALL: CASTLECARY

E of Castlecary village on B816 Cumbernauld to Bonnybridge road.
65 NS 790 783.
The low earthworks of a fort.

2. ANTONINE WALL: SEABEGS WOOD

1M W of Bonnybridge, access from the B816 on Castlecary to Bonnybridge road.
65 NS 811 792 - 818 792.
A stretch of rampart and ditch with the military way behind.

3. ANTONINE WALL: ROUGH CASTLE

Signposted at Bonnybridge. Signposted from the B816 between Bonnybridge and High Bonnybridge.
65 NS 835 798 - 845 799.
The best-preserved length of rampart and ditch, together with the earthworks of a fort – the most complete on the Wall – and a short length of military way with quarry pits. This is the best site to gain an impression of how the frontier and its integral forts worked.

4. AND 5. ANTONINE WALL: WATLING LODGE (EAST AND WEST)

In Falkirk, signposted from A9, access from the B816 from Tamforhill.
65 NS 863 798 - 866 798.
Two sections on each side of the house known as Watling Lodge (there is no entry to the house or grounds). The eastern section is one of the deepest and steepest stretches of the ditch visible.

6. ARDCHATTAN PRIORY

On Loch Etive, 6.5M NE of Oban off the A828. 49 NM 971 349.

The ruins of a Valliscaulian priory founded in 1230 and later converted to secular use.

7. BLACKNESS CASTLE

4M N of Linlithgow, on the Firth of Forth, off the A904. 65 NT 055 803.

Built in the 1440s, and massively strengthened in the 16th century as an artillery fortress, Blackness became an ammunition depot in the 1870s. The Office of Works restored it in the 1920s. Closed Thursday afternoons and Fridays in winter. Tel: 01506 834807.

★★★★ Grading.
Admission: Adult £2.20 Child 75p
Reduced £1.60.

P WC ☕ S ♿ £

8. BONAWE IRON FURNACE

Situated between the S shores of Loch Etive and the village of Taynuilt off the A85. NN 010 318.

Founded in 1753 by a Lake District partnership, this is the most complete charcoal fuelled ironworks in Britain. Displays illustrate how iron was made here in a beautiful Lochside setting. Open summer only. Tel: 01866 822432.

★★★★ Grading.
Admission; Adult £2.80 Child £1.00
Reduced £2.00. Joint ticket with Dunstaffnage Castle and Chapel available: Adult £4.00 Child £1.25
Reduced £3.00.

P WC 📷 ♿ ♿ ♨ £

9. CAMBUSKENNETH ABBEY

1M E of Stirling off the A907. 57 NS 809 939.

In its day the abbey was a famous house of Augustinian canons, the scene of Robert Bruce's Parliament in 1326, and burial place of James III and his Queen. The fine detached tower is the only substantial survivor, but extensive foundations remain of the other buildings. View exterior only. Open Summer only, keys available locally during the standard opening times published in this guide.

👞

10. CARNASSERIE CASTLE

2M N of Kilmartin off the A816. 55 NM 838 009.

A handsome combined tower house and hall, home of John Carswell, first Protestant Bishop of the Isles and translator of the first book printed in Gaelic. Very fine architectural details of the late 16th century.

👞

8.

11.

11. CASTLE CAMPBELL AND GARDEN

At the head of Dollar Glen, 10M E of Stirling on the A91 in Dollar. Parking is available in three car parks at the top, middle and bottom of the glen. NS 961 993.

Formerly known as the 'Castle of Gloom', this castle is beautifully sited. The oldest part is a well-preserved 15th-century tower around which other buildings were constructed, including an unusual loggia. Closed Thursday afternoons, Fridays and Sunday mornings in winter.
Tel: 01259 /42408.
★★★ Grading.
Admission: Adult £2.80 Child £1.00 Reduced £2.00.

P WC ☕ S ♨

12. CASTLE SWEEN

On the E shore of Loch Sween, in Knapdale off the B8025. 62 NR 712788.

This is one of the earliest castles in Scotland, dating to the 12th century. Later towers were built in addition to now vanished wooden structures.

13. CLACKMANNAN TOWER

In Clackmannan village near Alloa off the A907. NS 905 920.

A fine 14th-century keep enlarged in the 15th century. View exterior only.

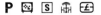

14. DOUNE CASTLE

In Doune off the A820.
NN 725 014 – 730 001

A magnificent late 14th-century courtyard castle built for the Regent Albany. Its most striking feature is the combination of tower, gatehouse and hall with its kitchen in a massive frontal block. Closed Thursdays and Fridays in winter.
Tel: 01786 841742.
★★★ Grading.
Admission: Adult £2.80 Child £1.00 Reduced £2.00.

P ▨ S ♨ ♨

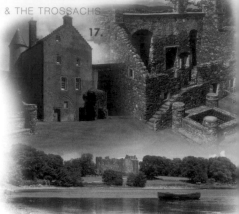

15. DUMBARTON CASTLE

In Dumbarton on the A82.
NS 398 744 – NS 401 745.

Spectacularly situated on a volcanic rock the castle is on the site of the ancient capital of Strathclyde. The most interesting features are the 18th-century artillery fortifications, with 19th-century guns. Closed Thursday afternoons and Fridays in winter. Tel: 01389 732167.

Admission: Adult £2.20 Child 75p
Reduced £1.60.
★★★★ Grading.

P [WC] [&] [🍴] [S] [£]

15.

16. DUNBLANE CATHEDRAL

In Dunblane just off the B8033.
NN 782 014.

One of Scotland's noblest medieval churches. The lower part of the tower is Romanesque, but the larger part of the building is of the 13th century. Sir Rowand Anderson restored the Cathedral in 1889-93. Open to visitors on Sundays from 1.30pm.

17. AND 18. DUNSTAFFNAGE CASTLE AND CHAPEL

By the village of Dunbeg off the A85, 3M N of Oban. 49 NM 882 344.

A fine 13th-century castle, built on a rock, with nearby ruins of a chapel of exceptional architectural refinement. Flora MacDonald was imprisoned here in 1746. Closed all day Thursday and Friday in winter. Sunday morning open 9.30am all year. Tel: 01631 562465.

★★★★ Grading.
Admission: Adult £2.20 Child 75p Reduced £1.60. Joint ticket with Bonawe Iron Furnace available: Adult £4.00 Child £1.20 Reduced £3.00.

P [🚌] [WC] [S] [&WC] [£]

19. EILEACH AN NAOIMH

An island in the Garvellach group, N of Jura. NM 637 096.

The ruins of Early Christian beehive cells, a chapel and a graveyard. The site is associated with St Brendan the Navigator.

🥾

20. EILEAN MOR: ST CORMAC'S CHAPEL

On an islet off the coast of Knapdale. 62 NR 666 753.

A chapel with a vaulted chancel containing the effigy of an ecclesiastical figure, probably of 12th-century date. Shaft of early medieval cross.

🥾

23.

21. INCHKENNETH CHAPEL

On an island on the west side of Mull.
48 NM 437 354.

A 13th-century chapel containing later
grave slabs of West Highland type.

22. INCHMAHOME PRIORY

On an island in the Lake of Menteith.
Reached by ferry from Port of Menteith
4M E of Abertoyle off the A81.
NN 574 005.

A beautifully situated Augustinian
monastery founded in 1238, with much
13th-century building surviving. Mary
Queen of Scots lived here briefly as an
infant. Open summer only.
Tel: 01877 385294.

★★★ Grading.
Admission: Adult £3.30 Child £1.20
Reduced £2.50. Ferry included in
admission price.

P [WC] [S] [㕣] [£]

23 AND 24. IONA ABBEY AND NUNNERY

On the island of Iona, public ferry from
Fionnphort, Mull, tel: 01681 700512.

Founded by St Columba in 563, the
restored abbey and monastic buildings
retain their spiritual atmosphere, and
house a superb collection of over 180
medieval carved stones, from high crosses
to pillow stones. The adjacent graveyard
has kings from Scotland, Norway, Ireland
and France buried there and is testimony
to the importance of the site. The nearby
remains of the 13th-century nunnery are
the idyllic location to experience the
tranquillity of this sacred isle. Open all
year, depending on ferries.

★★★★ Grading. Admission: Adult £2.80
Child £1.20 Reduced £2.00.

[WC] [⊠] [☕] [S] [♿] [㕣] [£]

St Columba Centre

In Fionnphort, Mull 5 minutes walk from
the public ferry to Iona

A modern interpretation centre focusing
on the life and work of St Columba and
the religious community he founded on
Iona in 563. Open Summer only 11.00am
to 5.00pm daily. Other times by prior
arrangement with Iona Abbey.
Tel: 01681 700660.

P [🚌] [WC] [⊠] [☕] [S] [♿] [♿wc]

25. IONA, MACLEAN'S CROSS

48 NM 285 242.
A fine 15th-century free-standing cross.

22.

26. KEILLS CHAPEL

6M SW of Tayvallich off the B8025. 55 NR 690 806.

A small West Highland chapel housing a collection of 12th-century grave slabs and early medieval sculpture, including the Keills Cross.

🥾

27.

27. KILBERRY SCULPTURED STONES

At Kilberry Castle, 17M SSW of Lochgilphead on the west coast of Knapdale off the B8024. 62 NR 709 642.

A collection of late-medieval sculptured stones gathered from the Kilberry estate.

28. KILCHURN CASTLE

At the NE end of Loch Awe, 2.5M W of Dalmally off the A85. 50 NN 133 276.

A square tower, built by Sir Colin Campbell of Glenorchy c1550. Much enlarged in 1693 it incorporates the first purpose built barracks in Scotland. The substantial ruins are some of the most picturesque in the country with spectacular views down Loch Awe. Open summer only. Regular sailings to Kilchurn by steamer from Loch Awe Pier. Tel: ferry company 01838 200440/200449.

29. KILDALTON CROSS

On the island of Islay, N of Ardbeg off the A846. 60 NR 458 508.

The finest intact high cross in Scotland carved in the late 8th century.

KILMARTIN GLEN MONUMENTS (Nos 30-41)

These monuments form a remarkable group.

30. KILMARTIN GLEN: ACHNABRECK CUP AND RING MARKS

1.5M NW of Lochgilphead off the A816. 55 NR 856 906.

The exposed crest of a rocky ridge with well-preserved cup and ring marks of early prehistoric date.

🥾

31. KILMARTIN GLEN: BALLYGOWAN CUP AND RING MARKS

1M SW of Kilmartin off the A816. 55 NR 816 978.

Cup and ring marks on natural rock faces, of early prehistoric date.

🥾

32. KILMARTIN GLEN: BALUACHRAIG CUP AND RING MARKS

1M SSE of Kilmartin off the A816. 55 NR 831 969.

Several groups of early prehistoric cup and ring marks on natural rock faces. Close to Dunchraigaig cairn.

🥾

33. KILMARTIN GLEN: CAIRNBAAN CUP AND RING MARKS

200 yards NW of the Cairnbaan Hotel, situated at the junction of the A816 and B841. 55 NR 838 910.

Cup and ring marks on a natural rock surface of Bronze Age date.

🥾

34. KILMARTIN GLEN: DUNADD FORT

2M S of Kilmartin off the A816.
55 NR 837 936.

This spectacular site has been occupied since the Iron Age. The well-preserved hill fort was a stronghold of Dalriada, the kingdom of the Scotti. On top of the hill a footprint, a boar and an ogham inscription have been carved into the natural rock

35. KILMARTIN GLEN: DUNCHRAIGAIG CAIRN

1.25M S of Kilmartin off the A816.
55 NR 833 968.

A Bronze Age cairn excavated in the last century.

P

36. KILMARTIN GLEN: GLEBE CAIRN, KILMARTIN

At Kilmartin Glebe off the A816.
55 NR 832 989.

An early Bronze Age burial cairn, one element of the line of five large burial cairns along the valley floor, forming a linear cemetery.

37. KILMARTIN GLEN: KILMARTIN SCULPTURED STONES

In Kilmartin Churchyard in the village of Kilmartin on the A816.

Over two dozen carved West Highland grave slabs, now housed in a former mausoleum and the graveyard. Parish church contains early medieval and medieval crosses.

P

38. KILMARTIN GLEN: KILMICHAEL GLASSARY CUP AND RING MARKS

Near the schoolhouse, Kilmichael Glassary off the A816. 55 NR 857 934.

Early prehistoric cup and ring carvings on a natural rock outcrop.

39. KILMARTIN GLEN: NETHER LARGIE CAIRNS

Between Kilmartin and Nether Largie off the A816. 55 NR 830 983, 831 985, 828 979.

One Neolithic and two Bronze Age cairns. Access within the chamber of the north cairn, to see the axe carvings on a cist slab inside. These are all in the line of five large burial cairns along the valley floor, known as the linear cemetery.

40. KILMARTIN GLEN: RI CRUIN CAIRN

1M SW of Kilmartin off the A816.
55 NR 825 971.

A Bronze Age burial cairn with the covering removed to reveal three massive cists. There are axe heads carved on one of the cist slabs. This cairn is the southernmost cairn of the linear cemetery.

P

41. KILMARTIN GLEN: TEMPLE WOOD STONE CIRCLES

0.25M SW of Nether Largie off the A816.
55 NR 826 978.

A circle of upright stones, and the remains of an earlier circle. Dating to about 3000 BC and in use for at least 1000 years.

42. KILMODAN SCULPTURED STONES

At Clachan of Glendaruel, 8M N of Colintraive off the A886. 55 NR 995 862.

A group of West Highland carved grave slabs exhibited in a burial aisle within Kilmodan churchyard.

43. KILMORY KNAP CHAPEL

On the shore between Loch Sween and Loch Caolisport in South Knapdale off the B8025. 62 NR 703 752.

A small medieval chapel with a collection of typical West Highland grave slabs and some early medieval sculpture. In the church is Macmillan's Cross, a splendid piece of medieval carving.

44. KINNEIL HOUSE

On the western outskirts of Bo'ness. Off A904 follow signs for Kinneil Museum. 65 NS 982 805.

Set in a public park, the oldest part of the house is a 15th-century tower remodelled by the Earl of Arran between 1546 and 1550 and transformed into a stately home for the Dukes of Hamilton in the 1660s. The grounds contain the ruins of James Watt's cottage and the boiler of his Necomen Engine.

P

45. ROTHESAY CASTLE

In Rothesay, Isle of Bute. Ferry from Wemyss Bay on the A78. NS 088 645.

A remarkable 13th-century castle, circular in plan, with a 16th-century forework. A favourite residence of the Stewart kings. There is a video of the exciting history of Rothesay. Closed Thursday afternoons and Fridays in winter. Tel: 01700 502691.

★★★★ Grading.
Admission: Adult £2.20 Child 75p
Reduced £1.60.

46. ST BLANE'S CHURCH, KINGARTH

At the south end of the Isle of Bute. 63 NS 094 535.

A 12th-century Romanesque chapel set within an early Christian monastery. A charming, tranquil spot.

P

47. ST MARY'S CHAPEL, ROTHESAY

On the outskirts of Rothesay. 63 NS 086 636.

The late-medieval remains of the chancel of the Parish Church of St Mary, recently re-roofed to protect its fine tombs. Open 8.00am to 5.00pm, Monday to Sunday, April to September. Closed on Fridays from October to March.

48 AND 49. SKIPNESS CASTLE AND CHAPEL

S of the village of Skipness on the E coast of Kintyre off the B8001. 62 NR 908 578, 62 NR 910 575.

A fine 13th-century castle with a 16th-century tower house in one corner. The early 14th-century chapel lies near the seashore and holds a small collection of fine grave slabs.

P

45.

50. STIRLING CASTLE

At the top of Castle Wynd at the head of Stirling's historic old town off the M9. NS 788 911.

Without doubt one of the grandest of all Scottish castles, both in its situation on a commanding rock outcrop and in its architecture. The Great Hall and the Gatehouse of James IV, the marvellous Palace of James V, the Chapel Royal of James VI and the artillery fortifications of the 16th to 18th centuries are all of outstanding interest. The views from the castle rock are spectacular. The Great Hall has recently been restored to how it would have looked around 1500. Displays on castle's history, medieval kitchen and attractive cafe.
Tel: 01786 450000.

Open all year seven days a week. April to September 9.30am to 6.00pm. October to March 9.30am to 5.00pm. Last ticket sold 45 minutes before closing.
Admission: Adult £7.00 Child £2.00 Reduced £5.00.
★★★★★ Grading.
Green Tourism Silver Award

P 🚌 wc 🔲 ☕ S ♿ ⚐ £

51. STIRLING: ARGYLL'S LODGING

At the top of Castle Wynd, Stirling. Parking available at nearby Stirling Castle. NS 772 938.

A superb mansion built around an earlier core in about 1630 and further extended by the Earl of Argyll in the 1670s. It is the most impressive town house of its period in Scotland. The principal rooms are now restored as they were in 1680. Tel: 01786 461146. Open all year seven days a week. April to September 9.30am to 6.00pm. October to March 9.30am to 5.00pm. Last ticket sold 45 minutes before closing.

★★★★ Grading.
Admission: Adult £3.00 Child £1.20 Reduced £2.25.

P 🚌 wc 🔲 🏛 S ♿ £

50.

52. STIRLING: KING'S KNOT

Below castle rock, Stirling. NS 78 7941.
The earthworks of a splendid formal garden, possibly made in 1628 for Charles I.

53. STIRLING; MAR'S WARK

At the head of Castle Wynd. NS 792 936.
A remarkable Renaissance mansion built by The Earl of Mar, Regent for James VI in 1570 and later used as the town workhouse. It was never completed and now only the façade can be seen.

★★★★★ Grading.
Green Tourism Silver Award.

54. STIRLING OLD BRIDGE

On the River Forth off the M9 at Stirling. NS 707 945.
A handsome bridge built in the 15th or early 16th century. The southern arch was rebuilt in 1749 after it had been blown up during "The '45" to prevent the Jacobite army entering the town.

55. WESTQUARTER DOVECOT

At Westquarter, near Lauriston. Access off the A803 on the Linlithgow to Lauriston road into Westquarter, then into the west end of Dovecot Road. NS 913 787.
A handsome rectangular dovecot with a heraldic panel dated 1647 over the entrance doorway.

10.

13.

1.

4.

AYRSHIRE
& ARRAN

1. ARRAN: AUCHAGALLON STONE CIRCLE

4M N of Blackwaterfoot on the E side of Arran off the A841. 69 NR 893 346.

A Bronze Age kerb cairn surrounded by a circle of 15 standing stones.

2. ARRAN: CARN BAN

3.5M NE of Lagg on the W side of Arran off the A841. 69 NR 990 262.

One of the most famous of the Neolithic long cairns of south-west Scotland. Walk of four miles to site.

3. ARRAN: KILPATRICK DUN (OR CASHEL)

1M S of Blackwaterfoot on the W side of Arran off the A841. 69 NR 906 262.

The ruins of a circular drystone homestead of unknown date, with a more recent enclosure wall. Walk of half mile to site.

4. ARRAN: LOCHRANZA CASTLE

At the northern coast of Arran off the A841. NR 931 506.

A fine tower house, probably a 16th-century reconstruction of an earlier building. Keys available locally during the standard opening times published in this guide.

P

5. ARRAN: MACHRIE MOOR STONE CIRCLES

3M N of Blackwaterfoot on the W side of Arran off the A841. 69 NR 910 324.

The remains of five stone circles of Bronze Age date, one of the most important sites of its kind in Britain. One and a half mile walk to site.

6. ARRAN: MOSS FARM ROAD STONE CIRCLE

3M N of Blackwaterfoot on the W side of Arran off the A841. 69 NR 900 326.

The remains of a Bronze Age cairn surrounded by a stone circle.

7. ARRAN: TORR A'CHAISTEAL FORT

4M N of Blackwaterfoot on the SW side of Arran off the A841. 69 NR 921 232.

A circular Iron Age fort on a ridge.

8. ARRAN: TORRYLIN CAIRN

0.25M SE of Lagg on the S side of Arran off the A841. 69 NR 955 210.

A Neolithic chambered cairn, with four compartments visible.

9. CASTLE SEMPLE COLLEGIATE CHURCH

2M W of Howwood on the B787 then on to the B776. 63 NS 377 601.

A late Gothic church, with a three-sided east end with windows of unusual style.

10. CROSSRAGUEL ABBEY

2M S of Maybole on the A77. 76 NS 275 083.

Founded in the early 13th century by the Earl of Carrick, this Cluniac abbey was much rebuilt during the next three centuries. The remains, which are remarkably complete and of a very high quality, include the church, cloister, chapter house and much of the domestic premises. The sacristy houses an exhibition on medieval building techniques. Open summer only. Tel: 01655 883113.

★★★ Grading.
Admission: Adult £2.00 Child 75p
Reduced £1.50.

P 🚌 WC 🚻 🔋 £

11. DUNDONALD CASTLE

In Dundonald village on the A71, 12M from Ayr and 5M from Kilmarnock. Leave A77 on to the B730 and follow signs for Dundonald. NS 363 345.

A prominent large stone castle overlooking the village, built by the first of the Stewart Kings, Robert II in the 1370s. Two great feasting halls, one above the other, with great vaults beneath. Remains of an earlier but equally grand 13th-century castle of the Stewarts are visible. Archaeological excavations have shown that the castle hill was occupied by a large fort in the Dark Ages and a prehistoric hill fort before that. Managed by the Friends of Dundonald Castle. Open seven days a week from April to October 10.00am to 5.00pm. Tel: 01563 850201.

★★★★ Grading.
Admission: Adult £2.00 Child £1.00
Reduced £1.00.

P 🚌 WC 🔋 🍴 🔋 S £

11.

44

12. KILWINNING ABBEY

In Kilwinning. Off A78 Kilwinning to Ardrossan road. NS 303 433.

The much-reduced remains of a Tironensian-Benedictine abbey, established from Kelso. Most of the surviving fragments, which consist of parts of the abbey church and chapter house, are of 13th-century date.

P

13. LARGS OLD KIRK

In Largs on the A78. Signed from the High Street. NS 202 594.

This jewel-like monument was erected in 1636 for Sir Robert Montgomerie of Skelmorlie. Contains an elaborate carved stone tomb in Renaissance style and a painted timber ceiling, with lively scenes illustrating the seasons. Open late May to early September from 2.00pm to 5.00pm. The key can be collected from the Largs Museum, tel: 01475 672450.

14. LOCH DOON CASTLE

Turn right 2M S of Dalmellington on the A713 on to an unclassified road signed for Loch Doon. 77 NX 484 950.

Transplanted in the mid-1930s from an island in the middle of Loch Doon due to a hydro electric scheme. The castle consists of an eleven-sided curtain wall, of fine masonry, dating from 1300.

P

15. MAYBOLE COLLEGIATE CHURCH

In Maybole on the A77. Left at crossroads in town centre and then first right. NS 301 098.

The chapel of St Mary was founded by John Kennedy of Dunure in 1371 and the associated college 11 years later. Its function was to allow prayers to be said for the founder and his family.

20.

1.

22.

12.

7.

3.

HIGHLANDS

1. ARDCLACH BELL TOWER

9M S of Nairn. Signposted off the A939 to Grantown on Spey. 27 NH 953 453.

A remarkable little fortified bell tower built in 1655 on the hill above the parish church of Ardclach. Tel: 01667 460232.

2. BEAULY PRIORY

In Beauly on the A862. 26 NH 527 464.

The ruined church of a Valliscaulian priory, one of three founded in 1230. Part of the building was later rebuilt in the 1530s. Open 11 June to 30 September, Monday to Sunday 9.30am to 6.30pm. Tel: 01667 460232.

P

3. BRIDGE OF OICH

4M S of Fort Augustus on the A82. 34 NH 338 035.

James Dredge designed this splendid suspension bridge in 1854. It was built using a sophisticated patented design of double cantilevered chain construction with massive granite pylon arches at either end. Tel: 01667 460232.

4. CAIRN O'GET

1.5M SW of Ulbster on the A9. 0.75M from car park to site via black and white poles. 12 ND 313 411.

A horned and chambered burial cairn of Neolithic date, located in an area of much archaeological interest. Access can be wet Tel: 01667 460232.

5. CARN LIATH

By the A9, 3M ENE of Golspie. 17 NC 870 013.

A typical Sutherland broch, surviving to first-floor level, with associated settlement. Tel: 01667 460232.

P

6. CASTLE OF OLD WICK

1M S of Wick on Shore Road. 12 ND 368 487.

The ruin of the best-preserved Norse castle in Scotland. Dating from the 12th-century this spectacular site is on a spine of rock projecting into the sea, between two deep, narrow gullies. Visitors must take great care. Tel: 01667 460232.

7. CLAVA CAIRNS

6M E of Inverness. Signposted from the B9091, 300 yards E of Culloden Battlefield. 27 NH 752 439.

A well-preserved Bronze Age cemetery complex of passage graves, ring cairns, kerb cairn and standing stones in a beautiful setting. In addition, the remains of a chapel of unknown date. Tel: 01667 460232.

P 🚌

8. CNOC FREICEADAIN LONG CAIRNS

6M WSW of Thurso on A836. 11 ND 013 654.

Two unexcavated long-horned burial cairns of Neolithic date, set at right angles to each other. Tel: 01667 460232.

👞

9. CORRIMONY CHAMBERED CAIRN

In Glen Urquhart, 8.5M W of Drumnadrochit off the A831. 26 NH 383 303.

An excavated passage grave of probable Bronze Age date, defined by a stone kerb and surrounded by a circle of 11 standing stones. Tel: 01667 460232.

10. DUN BEAG

0.25M W of Bracadale, Skye off the A863. 32 NG 339 385.

A fine example of a Hebridean broch, apparently occupied to the 18th century. Tel: 01667 460232.

P 👞

11. DUN DORNAIGIL

10M S of Hope, Sutherland off the A838. 9 NC 457 450.

Also known as Dun Dornadilla, a well-preserved broch with a distinctive enterance, standing to a height of up to 6.7 metres. Tel: 01667 460232.

P

12. FORT GEORGE

11M NE of Inverness. Near the village of Ardersier on the B9006. Signposted from the A96 at the Gollanfield junction. 27 NH 727 565.

A vast site and one of the most outstanding artillery fortifications in Europe. It was planned in 1747 as a base for George II's army and was completed in 1769. Since then it has served as a barracks. It is virtually unaltered and presents a complete view of the defensive system of an 18th-century artillery fort. Reconstruction of barrack rooms in different periods and the Seafield Collection - a display of muskets and pikes. Tel: 01667 462777.

★★★★ Grading.
Admission: Adult £5.00 Child £1.50 Reduced £3.50.

P 🚌 🚾 🍽 🥄 🍵 Ⓢ ♿ 🚾 🚻 💷

13. FORTROSE CATHEDRAL

In Fortrose on the A832. 27 NH 727 565.

The south aisle of the nave and chapter house survive at this beautiful red sandstone cathedral at Fortrose. Keys available locally during the standard opening times published in this guide. Tel: 01667 460232.

P

14. GLENELG BROCHS: DUN TELVE AND DUN TRODDAN

About 8M SE of Kyle of Lochalsh. Turn off at Shielbridge on the A87 onto unclassified road to Glenelg. 33 NG 829 172.

Two broch towers, standing more than 10 metres high, with well preserved structural features. Set in beautiful surroundings. Tel: 01667 460232.

👞

15. GREY CAIRNS OF CAMSTER

5M N of Lybster on the A9. Monument situated 5M along unclassified road. 11 ND 260 441.

Two chambered burial cairns of Neolithic date. One is long, with two chambers and projecting 'horns' and the other is round, and contains a single chamber. Access to chambers. Tel: 01667 460232.

P

16. HILL O' MANY STANES

At Mid Clyth, 4M NE of Lybster on A9. 11 ND 295 384.

More than 22 rows of low slabs arranged in a slightly fan-shaped pattern, which may have been a prehistoric astronomical observatory. Tel: 01667 460232.

17. HILTON OF CADBOLL CHAPEL

In village of Hilton off the B9166, 12M NE of Invergordon. 21 NH 873 768.

The foundations of a small rectangular chapel and, nearby, a modern carved reconstruction of the famous Pictish cross-slab found on the site and now in the National Museums of Scotland. Tel: 01667 460232.

18. INVERLOCHY CASTLE

2M NE of Fort William off the A82. 41 NN 121 755.

A fine well-preserved 13th-century castle of the Comyn family; in the form of a square, with round towers at the corners. The largest tower was the donjon or keep. It is one of Scotland's earliest stone castles.

P

19. KNOCKNAGAEL BOAR STONE

In The Highland Council Offices, Glenurquhart Road, Inverness on the A82. NH 657 413.

A rough slab incised with the Pictish symbols of a mirror-case and a wild boar.

Available during Council Office opening hours of 9.30am to 4.30pm, Monday to Friday. Tel: 01667 460232.

20. RUTHVEN BARRACKS

1M from Kingussie. Signposted from the A9 and the A86 in the centre of Kingussie. 35 NN 764 997.

An infantry barracks erected in 1719 following the Jacobite rising of 1715, with two ranges of quarters and a stable block. Captured and burnt by Prince Charles Edward Stuart's army in 1746. Tel: 01667 460232.

P

21. ST MARY'S CHAPEL, CROSSKIRK

6M W of Thurso on the A836. 12 ND 025 701.

A simple dry-stone chapel, probably of 12th-century date. Access can be muddy. Tel: 01667 460232.

P

22. URQUHART CASTLE

2M S of Drumnadrochit on the A82. 35 NH 531 286.

Magnificently sited, overlooking Loch Ness. Urquhart is one of the largest castles in Scotland, with a long and colourful history, built in the 1230s, seized by the English in 1296, sacked by the MacDonald Lord of the Isles in 1545 and left to fall into decay after 1689. Most of the existing buildings date from the 14th century and include the Grant Tower (16th century) the best-preserved part of the complex. New visitor centre with interpretation, audio-visual, shop and café. Sunday morning open 9.30am all year. Tel: 01456 450551. Coach times available from the operator on 08705 505050.

★★★★ Grading.
Admission: Adult £5.00 Child £1.20 Reduced £3.75.

P

WESTERN ISLES

Port of Ness

Stornoway

Tarbert

Rodel

Lochmaddy

Lochboisdale

Castlebay

1. BLACK HOUSE COMPLEX, ARNOL

In Arnol village, Lewis off the A858.
8 MB 310 492.

A traditional Lewis thatched house, with byre and stackyard, 1920s white house, complete and furnished, and consolidated ruin of a black house. Open all year except Sunday. Tel: 01851 710395.

★★★★★ Grading.
Admission: Adult £2.80 Child £1.00
Reduced £2.00.

2. CALANAIS STANDING STONES AND VISITOR CENTRE

About 12M W of Stornoway, Lewis off the A858. 8 NB 213 330.

A cross-shaped setting of standing stones, unique in Scotland and outstanding in Great Britain. Dates to around 2,900-2,600BC. The Urras nan Tursachan manages the visitor centre. Site open all year seven days a week. Visitor Centre closed Sunday. Open in summer from 10.00am-7.00pm and from 10.00am-4.00pm in winter. Tel: 01851 621422.

3. DUN CARLOWAY

1.5M S of Carloway, about 16m NW of Stornoway, Lewis on the A858.
NB 189 412.

One of the best preserved broch towers in Scotland. Visitor Centre managed by Urras nan Tursachan.

4. KISIMUL CASTLE

On the Island of Barra 0.25M from
Castlebay. Ferry Information from
Caledonian MacBrayne Ltd, tel: 01463
717680. 31 NL 665 979

The only surviving medieval castle in the
Western Isles. It is the Seat of the Chiefs to
the Clan Macneil. Complete with great
hall, kitchen, chapel, dungeon and 60-foot
tower. Extensive 20th-century rebuild as
former family home. Tel: 01871 810313.

Open summer from 9.30am to 6.30pm.
Adverse weather conditions may affect
ferry operations.
Admission: Adult £3.00 Child £1.00
Reduced £2.30.

S £

4.

5. ST CLEMENT'S CHURCH

At Rodel, Harris on the A859.
18 NG 046 831.

A fine 16th-century church, built by the
eighth chief MacLeod of Dunvegan and
Harris and containing his richly-carved
tomb.

6. STEINACLEIT CAIRN AND STONE CIRCLE

On the south end of Loch an Duin,
Shader, Lewis, NW of Stornoway on the
A857 to Ness. Access can be muddy.
8 NB 396 540.

The remains of an enigmatic structure of
early prehistoric date.

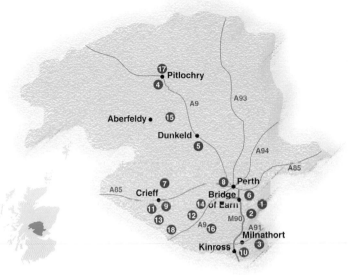

PERTHSHIRE

1. ABERNETHY ROUND TOWER

In the village of Abernethy off the A913 just E of the Bridge of Earn.
58 NO 192 163.

One of the two round towers of Irish style surviving in Scotland, dating from the end of the 11th century. Pictish symbol stone built into the tower. Fine views from the top. Open summer only during the standard opening times published in this guide.

2. BALVAIRD CASTLE

About 6M SE of Bridge of Earn off the A912. 58 NO 169 115.

A late 15th-century tower on an L plan, extended in 1581 by the addition of a walled courtyard and gatehouse. Refined architectural details. Limited opening, confirm by telephone: 01786 431324.

P 🚌

3. BURLEIGH CASTLE

0.5M E of Milnathort on the A911.
58 NO 128 045.

The roofless but otherwise complete ruin of a tower house of about 1500, with a section of defensive barmkin wall and a remarkable corner tower with a square cap-house corbelled out. Much visited by James IV. Keys available locally during the standard opening times published in this guide.

4. DUNFALLANDY STONE

1M S of Pitlochry off the A9. Not signposted. 55 NN 946 564.

An exceptionally well-preserved Pictish cross-slab with ornate decoration including human figures, Pictish symbols, zoomorphic designs and interlace. Covered by a protective enclosure.

🥾

5. DUNKELD CATHEDRAL

In the village of Dunkeld off the A9.
Beautifully situated on the banks of the Tay. The choir is now the parish church, but the 15th-century nave and the tower are cared for by Historic Scotland on behalf of Scottish Ministers.

6. ELCHO CASTLE

On the shores of the Tay 5M N of Bridge of Earn off the A912. 53 NO 164 210.
A handsome and complete fortified mansion of 16th-century date, with three projecting towers. The original wrought-iron grilles to protect the windows are still in place. Open summer only.
Tel: 01738 639998.

★★★★ Grading.
Admission: Adult £2.00 Child 75p
Reduced £1.50

7. FOWLIS WESTER SCULPTURED STONE

At Fowlis Wester, 6M NE of Crieff off the A85. 58 NN 927 240.
A tall cross-slab with Pictish symbols, figural scenes and ornate decoration. The original is now in the village church; a replica stands in the square.

8. HUNTINGTOWER CASTLE

2M W of Perth off the A85 Crieff road. 53 NO 082 251.
Two fine and complete towers, built in the 15th and 16th centuries and joined by a range in the 17th century. There is a fine painted ceiling in the hall of the eastern tower. Closed Thursday afternoons and Fridays in winter. Tel: 01738 627231.

★★★★ Grading.
Admission: Adult £2.20 Child 75p
Reduced £1.60

9. INNERPEFFRAY CHAPEL

Off the B8062 midway between Crieff and Auchterarder 58 NN 902 183.
A rectangular collegiate church founded in 1508. Still retains its altar, evidence of its furnishings and some painted details.

10.

10. LOCHLEVEN CASTLE

On an island in Loch Leven, accessible by boat from Kirkgate Park in Kinross, signposted from the A922. NO 137 017.
A late 14th or early 15th-century tower on one side of an irregular courtyard. Mary Queen of Scots was imprisoned here in 1567 but escaped the following year. Open summer only. Tel: 07778 040483.

★★★★ Grading.
Admission: Adult £3.30 Child £1.20
Reduced £2.50. Ferry included in admission price.

8.

11. MUTHILL OLD CHURCH AND TOWER

In Muthill, 3M SW of Crieff off the A822. NN 867 170.

The interesting ruins of an important medieval parish church. At its west end is a tall Romanesque tower. The remainder of the church is mostly of 15th-century date.

ROMAN SITES (Nos 12-14)

12. ROMAN SITE: ARDUNIE ROMAN SIGNAL STATION

Accessed by footpath 1M NW of the village of Denfield on the Trinity Gask road off the B8062 Crieff to Auchterarder road, not signposted. 58 NN 946 187.

The site of a Roman watch tower, one of a series running between Ardoch and the Tay, along the Gask Ridge dating to the first century.

13. ROMAN SITE: BLACKHILL CAMP

0.5m N of Braco off the A822 Crieff road just past the junction with the B827 Comrie road, not signposted. 58 NN 840 109.

Parts of the defences of two Roman marching camps, probably dating to the early third century.

14. ROMAN SITE: MUIR O' FAULD ROMAN SIGNAL STATION

Accessed by woodland footpath 1M NE of Trinity Gask off the B8062 Crieff to Auchterarder road, not signposted. 58 NN 982 189.

The site of a 1st-century Roman watch tower on the Gask Ridge.

15. ST MARY'S CHURCH, GRANDTULLY

3M NE of Aberfeldy off the A827. 52 NN 886 505.

A 16th century parish church, with a finely painted wooden ceiling illustrating heraldic and symbolic subjects, added in the 1630s.

P

16. ST SERF'S CHURCH, DUNNING

In Dunning village on the B9141 from the A9. NO 019 144.

The parish church of Dunning, with a square Romanesque tower and a splendid leading arch from the nave into the base of the tower. The body of the church was rebuilt in 1810 but still contains some of the original fabric. The 9th-century Dupplin Cross will move here in 2002. Keys available locally during the standard opening times published in this guide.

17. SUNNYBRAE COTTAGE

High Street, Pitlochry on the A924. The northernmost house.

This modest cottage is possibly the oldest house in Pitlochry. Sunnybrae Cottage is a rare survival of a type of house that was once very common in the Highlands, remarkably it still has the remains of a cruck framed roof construction, with most of its last thatch still surviving beneath the later corrugated iron roof. The cottage is currently undergoing careful recording and investigation. Access is restricted to exterior views during initial development work to prepare the property for visitors.

18. TULLIBARDINE CHAPEL

2M NW of Auchterarder off the A823 Crieff road. 58 NN 909 134.

One of the most complete and unaltered small medieval churches in Scotland, founded in 1446 and largely rebuilt about 1500. Much architectural detail has survived. Open summer only.

13.

8.

4.

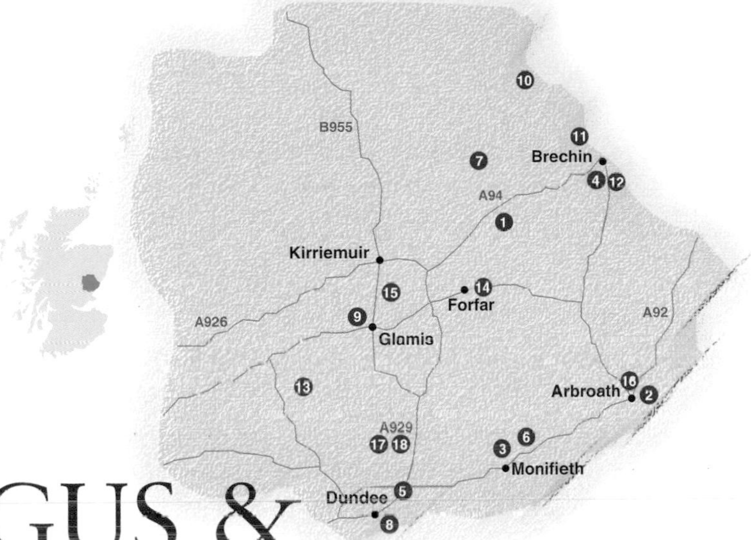

B955

10

B955

7 Brechin
4 12

A94

1

Kirriemuir

15 14
Forfar

11

A926

9

Glamis

A92

13

Arbroath 16
2

A929

17 18

3 6

•Monifieth

Dundee 5

8

ANGUS &
CITY OF DUNDEE

1. ABERLEMNO SCULPTURED STONES

On the B9134 in Aberlemno village 6M NE of Forfar. NO 522 555/NO 522 558/NO 522 559.

Magnificent range of Pictish sculptured stones: three stand alongside the B9134 and one, a cross-slab with interlaced decoration, Pictish symbols and a battle scene is in the churchyard. All are covered in winter to protect them from the elements.

2. ARBROATH ABBEY

In Arbroath town centre just off the A92. NO 643 413.

The substantial ruins of a Tironensian monastery, founded by William the Lion in 1178 who is buried in the Abbey. Parts of the abbey church and domestic buildings remain, notably the gatehouse range and the abbot's house. The Abbey is famously associated with the *Declaration of Arbroath* of 1320, which asserted Scotland's independence from England. New visitor centre and enhanced interpretation. Tel: 01241 878756.

★★★ Grading.
Admission: Adult £2.50 Child 75p
Reduced £1.90.

▢ ▢ ▢

3. ARDESTIE EARTH-HOUSE

1.25M N of Monifieth off the A92. 54 NO 502 344.

A curved underground gallery 80 feet in length of Iron Age date, now uncovered, that once formed the cellar of a round house.

4. BRECHIN CATHEDRAL ROUND TOWER

In Brechin town centre off the A933. NO 596 600.

One of the two remaining round towers of the Irish type in Scotland, built in the late 11th century with a remarkable carved doorway. Capped by a stone roof added in the 15th century. View exterior of the tower, but the adjacent church houses a magnificent collection of carved stones.

5. BROUGHTY CASTLE

On the shores of the Tay in Broughty Ferry off the A930. 54 NO 465 304.

Originally built in the late 15th century, Broughty Castle was adapted through the centuries to meet the nation's changing defence needs. The castle has stunning views over the Tay. It now houses a museum run by Dundee City Council. Tel: 01382 436916.

6. CARLUNGIE EARTH-HOUSE

2.5M NNE of Monifieth off the B978. 54 NO 511 359.

A complex underground structure, 150 feet long, of Iron Age date. Now uncovered.

7. CATERTHUNS (BROWN AND WHITE)

About 5M E of the village of Inchbare off the B966 Brechin to Edzell road. 44 NO 555 668, 44 NO 547 660.

Two spectacularly large hill forts. The Brown Caterthun is defended by four earth ramparts and ditches, and the White has a massive stone rampart, a ditch and outer ramparts.

8. CLAYPOTTS CASTLE

Off the A92 E of Dundee at Claypotts Junction. 54 NO 457 319.

An outstanding example of 16th-century Scottish architecture, which is both intact and little altered. The castle owes its striking appearance to asymmetrical square garrett chambers corbelled out over two circular towers at diagonally opposite corners. Built by John Strachan between 1569 and 1588, and later owned by 'Bonnie Dundee', John Graham of Claverhouse, it was inhabited into the 19th century. Limited opening, confirm by telephone: 01786 431324.

9. EASSIE SCULPTURED STONE

In the old church of Eassie, W of Glamis off the A94. 54 NO 352 474.

An elaborately sculptured Pictish cross-slab with an intricate cross, angels, animals, warrior, Pictish symbols and three hooded figures. Covered by a protective enclosure.

10.

10. EDZELL CASTLE AND GARDEN

Near Edzell village off the B966, 6M N of Brechin.

A remarkable and very beautiful complex with a late medieval tower house incorporated into a 16th-century courtyard mansion, and a walled garden with a bathhouse and summer house originally laid out in 1604. The carved decoration of the garden walls is unique in Britain. Closed Thursday afternoons and Fridays in winter. Tel: 01356 648631.

★★★★ Grading.
Admission: Adult £2.80 Child £1.00 Reduced £2.00.

11. LINDSAY BURIAL AISLE

In Edzell graveyard off the B9661, 6M north of Brechin. 44 NO 582 688.

This small burial Aisle is all that remains of the 14th-century Edzell Old Church. The Aisle was built by the Lindsays of Edzell as a chantry chapel in the 16th century and was later used as their burial vault. Closed Thursday afternoons and Fridays in winter. Tel: 01356 648631.

12. MAISON DIEU CHAPEL, BRECHIN

In Maison Dieu Lane, Brechin off the
B9134. Not signposted.

Part of the south wall of a chapel,
belonging to a medieval hospital founded
in the 1260s with finely-detailed doors and
windows.

13. MEIGLE SCULPTURED STONES

In the village of Meigle 5M NE of Coupar
Angus off the A94.

A magnificent collection of 26 sculptured
monuments, one of the most important
site-specific assemblages of early medieval
sculpture in Western Europe.
Open summer only. Tel: 01828 640612.

★★★ Grading.
Admission: Adult £2.00 Child 75p
Reduced £1.50.

14. RESTENNETH PRIORY

1M NE of Forfar off the B9134 Brechin
road. 54 NO 482 516.

The chancel and tower of the priory
church of Augustinian canons. The lower
part of the tower is very early Romanesque
work.

P

15. ST ORLAND'S STONE

In a field near Cossans farm, 4.5M W of
Forfar off the A926. 54 NO 400 500.

A tall, Pictish cross-slab with a prominent,
ornate cross and, on the reverse, Pictish
symbols, a hunting scene and a very rare
depiction of a boat.

16. ST VIGEANS SCULPTURED STONES

In the village of St Vigeans 0.5M N of
Arbroath off of the A92.

A fascinating and very important
collection of over 30 Pictish carved stones
housed in a cottage in the charming village
of St Vigeans. Open summer only. Keys
available locally during the standard
opening times published in this guide.

17 AND 18. TEALING DOVECOT AND EARTH HOUSE

Close to the village of Balgray 5M N of
Dundee off the A90. 54 NO 412 381.

An elegant dovecot of the late 16th century
standing in a modern farmyard. A short
walk leads to the remains of an earth
house, or souterrain, of Iron Age date, a
curving underground passage, now
uncovered. Re-used stones with Bronze
Age rock carvings can be seen in its walls.

13.

61

5.

21.

16.

22.

11.

17.

Map labels: 28 29 30 4 12 15 20 Fraserburgh, Banff, 10 A98 23, Forres, 8, Elgin, Fochabers, Peterhead, A96, 9, A941, A95, 2, Dufftown, Huntly, 17, A947, A92, 1, A941, 25, 21, 31 32, A96, 22, 3, A92, 27, Inverurie, 14, 16 18, Alford, 19, 13, A944, A944, 26, 5, 7, A980, 6, Aberdeen, 33 24, Draemar, A93, Aboyne, A94, A92

ABERDEEN & GRAMPIAN

1. AUCHINDOUN CASTLE

2M S of Dufftown on the A941.
28 NJ 348 376.

The castle crowns a lonely hilltop with dramatic views over the surrounding hills. It was built about 1480 by Thomas Cochrane, Earl of Mar and favourite of James III. It still retains fine architectural details and is surrounded by the ramparts of an Iron Age hillfort. Access on foot only, route is steep and can be wet at times. View exterior only. Tel: 01466 793191.

2. BALVENIE CASTLE

At Dufftown on the A941. 28 NJ 326 408.
A castle of enclosure first owned by the Comyns with a curtain wall of 13th-century date. Added to in the 15th and 16th centuries. Visited by Mary Queen of Scots in 1562. Open summer only
Tel: 01340 820121.

★★★★ Grading.
Admission: Adult £1.50 Child 50p
Reduced £1.10.

P WC S & ⌂ £

3. BRANDSBUTT SYMBOL STONE

About 1M NW of Inverurie off the A96.
38 NJ 759 224.

An early Pictish symbol stone, with an ogham inscription. Tel: 01466 793191.

4. BURGHEAD WELL

In King Street, Burghead on the B9013. Signposted at the north end of Grant Street in the village. 28 NJ 110691.

A rock-cut well, identified by some as an early Christian baptistry associated with the local cult of St Ethan.
Tel: 01667 460232.

5. CORGARFF CASTLE

8M W of Strathdon on the A939.
37 NJ 254 086.

A 16th-century tower house converted into a barracks for Government troops in 1748. Its last military use was to control the smuggling of illicit whisky between 1827 and 1831. Still complete and with its 18th-century star-shaped fortification. Open all summer and at weekends in winter.
Tel: 01975 651460.
Access is up a steep incline.

★★★★ Grading.
Admission: Adult £2.80 Child £1.00
Reduced £2.00.

P 🚌 ▦ S £

2.

63

6. CULLERLIE STONE CIRCLE

0.75M S of Garlogie off the B9125.
38 NJ 786 042.

A circle of eight stones enclosing an area consecrated by fires on which eight small cairns were later built. About 4000 years old. Tel: 01466 793191.

P

7. CULSH EARTH HOUSE

At Culsh, 1M E of Tarland on the B9119.
37 NJ 504 054.

A well-preserved underground passage, with roofing slabs intact over the large chamber and entrance. About 2000 years old. Tel: 01466 793191.

8. DALLAS DHU HISTORIC DISTILLERY

1M S of Forres off the A940 to Grantown on Spey. Also from the B9010 by following the Malt Whisky Trail signs.
27 NJ 035 566.

A perfectly preserved time capsule of the distiller's art. Built in 1898 to supply malt whisky for Wright and Greig's 'Roderick Dhu' blend. Audio-visual presentation and free audio guide. See and hear how whisky was made and sample a free dram. Closed Thursday afternoons and Fridays in winter. Tel: 01309 676548.

★★★★ Grading.
Admission: Adult £3.30 Child £1.00
Reduced £2.50.

P 🚐 📶 🏛 Ⓢ ♿ ♿ꟙ 🚻 💷

8.

9. DEER ABBEY

2M W of Mintlaw on the A950.
30 NJ 968 481.

The remains of a Cistercian monastery founded in 1219. Tel: 01466 793191

P

10. DESKFORD CHURCH

4M S of Cullen on the B9018 to Keith.
29 NJ 509 616.

The ruin of a small late medieval church with a richly carved sacrament house of a type characteristic of north-east Scotland. Tel: 01466 793191.

11. DUFF HOUSE

In Banff on the A96. 29 NJ 690 633.

A magnificent early Georgian mansion, designed by William Adam for the Earl of Fife and acknowledged to be Adam's masterpiece. Now open as a Country House Gallery of the National Galleries of Scotland. Open all summer 10.00am-5.00pm. Open Thursday to Sunday in winter 10.00am-5.00pm. Tel: 01261 818181.

(Historic Scotland Friends retail discount not eligible). Please telephone for admission prices.

P 🚐 📶 📶 ☕ Ⓢ ♿ ♿ꟙ 🚻 💷

12. DUFFUS CASTLE

5M NW of Elgin on the B9012 to Burghead. 28 NJ 189 672.

One of the finest examples of a motte and bailey castle in Scotland with a later, very fine, stone hall house and curtain wall. The original seat of the Moray family. Tel: 01667 460232

P 👞

13. DYCE SYMBOL STONES

Normally 0.75M N of Kirkton off Aberdeen Airport ring road but currently removed from site for conservation.
38 NJ 875 154.

Two Pictish stones, one with the older type of incised symbols and the other with symbols accompanied by a cross and decoration. Tel. 01466 793191.

P

14. EASTER AQUHORTHIES STONE CIRCLE

1M W of Inverurie on the A96.
38 NJ 732 207.

A recumbent stone circle about 4000 years old. Car parking nearby.
Tel: 01466 793191.

🐾

15. ELGIN CATHEDRAL

In Elgin on the A96. 28 NJ 222 630.

The superb ruin of what many think was Scotland's most beautiful cathedral. Much of the work is in a rich late 13th-century style, much modified after the burning of the church by the Wolf of Badenoch in 1390. The octagonal chapter house is the finest in Scotland. Also included within the area surrounding the Cathedral are the Bishop's House, the Pans Port and parts of the Cathedral precinct wall. Pictish cross-slab. Closed Thursday afternoons and Fridays in winter. Bishop's House view exterior only. Tel: 01343 547171.

★★★★ Grading.
Admission: Adult £2.80 Child £1.00 Reduced £2.00. Joint ticket with Spynie Palace available: Adult £3.00 Child £1.20 Reduced £2.50

🔣 S 🚹 ♿ 💷

16. GLENBUCHAT CASTLE

6M W of Kildrummy on the A97.
37 NJ 397 148.

A fine example of a Z-plan tower house, built in 1590. Its last laird, John Gordon, was a notable Jacobite. Tel: 01466 793191.

P 🐾

17. HUNTLY CASTLE

In Huntly signposted from the A96.
29 NJ 532 407.

A magnificent ruin of a castle from the 12th-century motte to the palace block erected in the 16th and 17th centuries by the Gordon family. The architectural details and heraldic enrichments are particularly impressive. Beautiful setting. Closed Thursday afternoons and Fridays in winter. Tel: 01466 793191.

★★★★ Grading.
Admission: Adult £3.00 Child £1.00 Reduced £2.20.

P 🚻 🔣 S ♿ 🚹 💷

15.

18. KILDRUMMY CASTLE

10M SW of Alford on the A97.
37 NJ 455 164.

Though ruined, a fine example of a 13th-century castle, with a curtain wall, four round towers, hall and chapel of that date. The seat of the Earls of Mar, it was dismantled after the first Jacobite rising in 1715. Open summer only.
Tel: 01975 571331.

★★★ Grading.
Admission: Adult £2.00 Child 75p
Reduced £1.50.

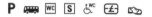

19. KINKELL CHURCH

2M S of Inverurie off the B993 to Whiterashes. Follow unclassified road to Mill of Fintray. 38 NJ 785 190.

The ruins of a 16th-century parish church, with fine sacrament house dated 1524, and the grave slab of Gilbert de Greenlaw, killed in battle in 1411. Tel: 01466 793191.

20. KINNAIRD HEAD CASTLE LIGHTHOUSE AND MUSEUM

On a promontory in Fraserburgh on the A92. 30 NJ 999 675.

This fine 16th-century castle built for the Fraser family was altered to take the first lighthouse built by the Commissioners of the Northern Lighthouses in 1787. It is still in working order but has now been replaced by a small unmanned light nearby. The lighthouse remains much as it was left by the last lighthouse crew. Managed by the Kinnaird Head Trust. Joint ticket with Scotland's National Lighthouse Museum. Open all year seven days a week. For further details, telephone: 01346 511022.

(Historic Scotland Friends retail discount not eligible). Please telephone for admission prices.

21. LOANHEAD STONE CIRCLE

Near Daviot, 5M NW of Inverurie off the A96. 38 NJ 747 288.

The best known of a group of recumbent stone circles, enclosing a ring cairn. Beside it is a small burial enclosure. From 4000-4500 years old. Tel: 01466 793191.

22. MAIDEN STONE

Near Chapel of Garioch, 4.5M NW of Inverurie on the A96. 38 NJ 703-247.

A Pictish cross-slab of 9th-century date, it bears on one side a cross and, on the other, a variety of Pictish symbols.
Tel: 01466 793191.

23. MEMSIE CAIRN

3.5M S of Fraserburgh on the A981 in Memsie Village. 30 NJ 976 620.

A large stone-built cairn, possibly of Bronze Age date, but enlarged during field clearance during the last two centuries.
Tel: 01466 793191

24. PEEL RING OF LUMPHANAN

0.5M SW of Lumphanan off the A980. 37 NJ 576 036.

This great earthwork of 13th-century date was the site of a fortified residence, perhaps a hunting lodge of the Durward family. Tel: 01466 793191.

25. PICARDY SYMBOL STONE

8M S of Huntly off the A96 to Raes of Inch (second road on the left). 29 NJ 609 302.

One of the oldest, simplest, Pictish symbol stones, possibly of 7th-century date.
Tel: 01466 793191.

26. ST MACHAR'S CATHEDRAL TRANSEPTS

In Old Aberdeen. 38 NJ 939 087.

The nave and towers of the Cathedral remain in use as a church, and the ruined transepts are in care. In the south transept is the fine tomb of Bishop Dunbar (1514-32). Tel: 01466 793191.

27. ST MARY'S KIRK, AUCHINDOIR

Off the A944 between villages of Rhynie and Lumsden on the B9002. 37 NJ 477 244.

One of the finest medieval parish churches in Scotland, roofless, but otherwise entire. There is a rich early Romanesque doorway and a beautiful early 14th-century sacrament house, comparable with those at Deskford and Kinkell. Tel: 01466 793191.

28. ST PETER'S KIRK AND PARISH CROSS, DUFFUS

0.5M E of village of Duffus. Signposted from the B9012 in the centre of the village. 28 NJ 175 686.

The roofless remains of the kirk include the base of a 14th-century western tower, a 16th-century vaulted porch and some interesting tombstones. The cross is of 14th-century date. Keys available locally during the standard opening times published in this guide. Tel: 01667 460232.

29. SPYNIE PALACE

2M N of Elgin off the A941 to Lossiemouth. 28 NJ 230 658.

The residence of the bishops of Moray from the 14th century to 1686. Dominated by the massive tower built by Bishop David Stewart (1461-77), with spectacular views over Spynie Loch. Open all summer and at weekends in winter. Tel: 01343 546358.

★★★★ Grading.
Admission: Adult £2.00 Child 75p Reduced £1.50. Joint ticket with Elgin Cathedral available: Adult £3.30 Child £1.20 Reduced £2.50.

P 🚌 WC S ♿ 🚻 £

30. SUENO'S STONE

At the E end of Forres off the A96. 27 NJ 046 595.

The most remarkable sculptured monument in Britain, probably a cenotaph, standing over 20 feet high and dating to the end of the first millennium AD. Covered by a protective glass enclosure. Tel: 01667 460232.

P

31. TARVES MEDIEVAL TOMB

In Tarves kirkyard, 15M NNW of Aberdeen on the A920. 30 NJ 871 313.

A fine altar tomb of William Forbes, the laird who enlarged Tolquhon Castle. The carving is a remarkable survival. Tel: 01466 793191.

32. TOLQUHON CASTLE

15M N from Aberdeen on the A920. 38 NJ 872 286.

Built for the Forbes family, Tolquhon has an early 15th-century tower, which was enlarged by William Forbes between 1584 and 1589 with a large mansion round a courtyard. Noted for its highly ornamented gatehouse, set within a barmkin with adjacent pleasance. Open all summer and at weekends in winter. Tel: 01651 851286.

★★★★ Grading.
Admission: Adult £2.00 Child 75p Reduced £1.50.

P 🚌 WC ♿ ♿ 🚻 £

33. TOMNAVERIE STONE CIRCLE

Near Mill of Wester Coull, about 3M NW of Aboyne on the B9094. 37 NJ 486 034.

A recumbent stone circle about 4000 years old. Tel: 01466 793191.

23.

1. & 2.

3.

ORKNEY

1 AND 2. BISHOP'S AND EARL'S PALACES, KIRKWALL

Situated on Palace Road opposite St Magnus Cathedral in Kirkwall on the A960. 6 HY 448 108.

The Bishop's Palace is a hall-house of 12th-century date, later much altered, with a round tower built by Bishop Reid in 1541-48. A later addition was made by the notorious Patrick Stewart, Earl of Orkney, who built the adjacent Earl's Palace between 1600 and 1607 in a splendid Renaissance style. Open summer only. Tel: 01856 875461.

★★★★ Grading.
Admission: Adult £2.00 Child 75p Reduced £1.50. Joint ticket available for all Orkney staffed monuments.

3. BLACKHAMMER CHAMBERED CAIRN

On B9064 on Island of Rousay 2M W of pier. Orkney Ferries Limited from Tingwall Terminal, tel: 01856 751360. 5 HY 414 276.

Neolithic burial cairn, similar in general shape and subdivisions to the contemporary Neolithic houses at Knap of Howar. Access to chamber.

1.

4. BROUGH OF BIRSAY

On a tidal island at Birsay, 20M NW of Kirkwall off the A966. Check tide tables at Skara Brae, tel: 01856 841815. 6 HY 239 285.

Pictish and Norse power-base with Pictish well, replica carving, extensive ruins of Norse houses and 12th-century church. Open when tides permit 11 June to 30 September, Monday to Sunday 9.30am to 6.30pm.

Admission: Adult £1.50 Child 50p Reduced £1.10. Joint ticket available for all Orkney staffed monuments. Telephone the Earl's Palace, Birsay 01856 721205.

5. BROCH OF GURNESS (AIKERNESS BROCH)

At Aikerness, 14M NW of Kirkwall on the A966. 6 HY 381 268.

Protected by three lines of ditch and rampart, the base of this broch is surrounded by a well organised Iron Age village. The internal fittings of all the buildings are of particular interest. Pictish house rebuilt to one side. Open summer only. Tel: 01856 751414.

★★★★ Grading.
Admission: Adult £2.80 Child £1.00 Reduced £2.00. Joint ticket available for all Orkney staffed monuments.

6. CLICK MILL, DOUNBY

2.5M from Dounby on the B905 to Evie village. 6 HY 325 228.

The last surviving horizontal water mill in Orkney, of a type well represented in Shetland and Lewis. In working order. Access can be muddy. Tel: 01856 841815.

7 AND 8. CUBBIE ROW'S CASTLE AND ST MARY'S CHAPEL

On the island of Wyre 0.5M from pier. Orkney Ferries Ltd from Kirkwall, tel: 01856 872044. 6 HY 442 264.

The castle is probably one of the earliest stone castles to survive in Scotland, built in about 1145 by the Norseman Kolbein Hruga. It is a small rectangular tower enclosed in a circular ditch. The ruined chapel is of late 12th-century date, in Romanesque style.

9. CUWEEN HILL CHAMBERED CAIRN

0.5M S of Finstown on B9056 from Kirkwall. 6 HY 364 128.

A low mound covering a Neolithic chambered tomb with four cells.

Contained the bones of men, dogs and oxen when discovered. Access to chambers. Access can be muddy. Tel: 01856 841815.

10. DWARFIE STANE

Towards the N end of Hoy, 3.5M from Rackwick. Orkney Ferries Ltd from Houton Terminal, tel: 01856 811397. 7 HY 244 005.

A huge block of sandstone in which a Neolithic burial chamber has been cut. Access to chambers. Tel: 01856 841815.

11 AND 12. EARL'S BU AND CHURCH, ORPHIR

8M WSW of Kirkwall on the A964 to Houton and Orphir. 6 HY 334 043.

The Earl's Bu is the name for the foundations of ancient buildings, which may be an Earl's residence of the Viking period. The church is of 12th-century date, and consists of the chancel and part of the nave of the only medieval round church in Scotland. Parking nearby. Tel: 01856 841815.

13. EARL'S PALACE, BIRSAY

In Birsay on the A966. 6 HY 248 277.

The gaunt remains of the residence of Robert Stewart, Earl of Orkney, constructed in the late 16th-century round a courtyard. Tel: 01856 721205 or 01856 841815.

14. EYNHALLOW CHURCH

On the island of Eynhallow. Can only be reached by private hire boat from mainland Orkney or Rousay. 6 HY 359 289.

Ruined 12th-century monastic church and post-medieval domestic buildings. Tel: 01856 841815.

15. GRAIN EARTH HOUSE

About 1M NW of Kirkwall in Hatston Industrial Estate off the A965.
6 HY 442 117.

A well-built Iron Age earth house of underground chamber supported on stone pillars.

16 AND 17. HACKNESS MARTELLO TOWER AND BATTERY

At the SE end of Hoy. Orkney Ferries Ltd from Houton Terminal, tel: 01856 811397.
/ ND 338 912.

One of a pair of towers built between 1813 and 1815 to provide defence against French and American privateers for British convoys assembling in the sound of Longhope. Provided a base for a 25-pounder cannon and its crew. The Battery is being actively conserved for future public presentation. Tel: 01856 841815.

18. HOLM OF PAPA WESTRAY CHAMBERED CAIRN

On the island of Holm of Papa Westray. Reached by private boat hire from Papa Westray. 5 HY 509 518.

A massive tomb with a long, narrow chamber divided into three, with 14 beehive cells opening into the walls. There are engravings on the walls. Access to chamber. Tel: 01856 841815.

19. KNAP OF HOWAR

On the island of Papa Westray about 0.25M W of Holland Farm. Orkney Ferries Ltd from Kirkwall, tel: 01856 872044.
6 HY 183 510.

Probably the oldest standing stone houses in north-west Europe, dating from the early Neolithic period. Two houses, approximately rectangular, with stone cupboards and stalls. Contemporary with the chambered tombs of Orkney.
Tel: 01856 841815.

20. KNOWE OF YARSO CHAMBERED CAIRN

On the island of Rousay on the B9064, 3M from pier. Orkney Ferries from Tingwall Terminal, tel: 01856 751 360.
5 HY 404 279.

An oval cairn with concentric walls enclosing a Neolithic chambered tomb divided into three compartments. Access to chamber. Tel: 01856 841815.

21. LINKS OF NOLTLAND

On the island of Westray. Orkney Ferries Ltd from Kirkwall, tel: 01856 872044.
5 HY 429 494.

Sand dunes seal and protect these significant prehistoric remains in a fragile environment requiring careful management. Little can be seen of the remains.

22. MAES HOWE CHAMBERED CAIRN

9M W of Kirkwall on the A965.
6 HY 318 128.

The finest megalithic tomb in the British Isles, with a large mound covering a stone-built passage and a large burial chamber with cells in the walls. Of Neolithic date, broken into in Viking times by people who carved extensive runic inscriptions on the walls. Part of The Heart of Neolithic Orkney World Heritage Site. Admission, shop and refreshments at the nearby 19th-century Tormiston Mill.
Tel: 01856 761606.

★★★★ Grading.
Admission: Adult £2.80 Child £1.00 Reduced £2.00. Joint ticket available for all Orkney staffed monuments.

22.

23. MIDHOWE BROCH

On the island of Rousay on the B9064, 5M from pier. Orkney Ferries Ltd from Tingwall Terminal, tel: 01856 751360. 6 HY 371 308.

A well-preserved broch, with remains of later buildings round it. As at Gurness, impressive evidence for the internal appearance of houses survives. Very steep access, follow the black and white poles. Tel: 01856 841815.

24. MIDHOWE CHAMBERED CAIRN

On the island of Rousay on the B9064, 5M from pier. Orkney Ferries Ltd from Tingwall Terminal, tel: 01856 751360. 6 HY 372 306.

A huge and impressive megalithic chambered tomb of Neolithic date in an oval mound, with 25 stalls. Now protected by a modern building. Very steep access, follow the black and white poles. Tel: 01856 841815.

25. NOLTLAND CASTLE

On the island of Westray, 1M W of Pierowall village. Orkney Ferries Ltd from Kirkwall, tel: 01856 872044. 5 HY 429 488.

A fine, ruined Z-plan tower, built between 1560 and 1573 but never completed. Remarkable for its large number of gun loops and impressive staircase. Open 11 June to 30 September, Monday to Sunday 9.30am to 6.30pm. Tel: 01856 841815.

26. PIEROWALL CHURCH

On the island of Westray in the village of Pierowall. Orkney Ferries Ltd from Kirkwall, tel: 01856 872044. 5 HY 438 487.

The ruins of a medieval church with some finely lettered tombstones. Tel: 01856 841815.

27. QUOYNESS CHAMBERED CAIRN

On the island of Sanday on the southern point of Els Ness, 2.5M from Kettlehoft village. Orkney Ferries Ltd from Kirkwall, tel: 01856 872044. 6 HY 677 378.

A megalithic tomb with triple retaining walls, containing a passage and main chamber, with six subsidiary cells. Of Neolithic date. Access to chambers. Tel: 01856 841815.

28. RENNIBISTER EARTH-HOUSE

About 4.5M WNW of Kirkwall on the A965. 6 HY 397 127.

A good example of an Orkney earth house, like that at Grain. Tel: 01856 841815.

29. RING OF BROGAR STONE CIRCLE AND HENGE

About 5M NE of Stromness on the B9055. 6 HY 294 134.

A magnificent circle of upright stones with an enclosing ditch spanned by causeways, dating to late Neolithic period. Part of The Heart of Neolithic Orkney World Heritage Site. Tel: 01856 841815.

P

30. ST MAGNUS CHURCH

On the island of Egilsay 0.5M from pier. Orkney Ferries Ltd from Tingwall Terminal, tel: 01856 751360. 6 HY 466 304.

The complete but roofless ruin of a 12th-century church with a round tower, dramatically sited. Tel: 01856 841815.

31. SKARA BRAE PREHISTORIC VILLAGE

19M NW of Kirkwall on the B9056. 6 HY 231 188.

The best preserved group of Stone Age houses in Western Europe. The houses contain stone furniture, hearths and drains and give a remarkable picture of life in Neolithic times. Part of The Heart of Neolithic Orkney World Heritage Site. Visitor centre with original artefacts and replica house. Tel: 01856 841815.

★★★★★ Grading.

Admission: Summer: (Joint ticket with the nearby Skaill House) Adult £4.50 Child £1.30 Reduced £3.30 Winter: (Skara Brae only) Adult £3.50 Child £1.20 Reduced £2.60. Joint ticket available for all Orkney staffed monuments.

P 🚌 ♿ ☕ 📖 £

32. STONES OF STENNESS CIRCLE AND HENGE

About 5M NE of Stromness on the B9055. 6 HY 306 126.

The remains of a stone circle surrounded by remains of a circular earthen bank. Tel: 01856 841815.

P 🚌

33. TAVERSÖE TUICK CHAMBERED CAIRN

On the island of Rousay 0.5M W of pier. Orkney Ferries Ltd from Tingwall Terminal, tel: 01856 751 360. 6 HY 426 276.

A Neolithic chambered cairn with unusual arrangement of two burial chambers, one above the other. Access to chambers. Access can be muddy. Tel: 01856 841815.

🥾

34. TORMISTON MILL

About 9M W of Kirkwall on the A965. 6 HY 322 127.

An excellent late example of a Scottish watermill. It was probably built in the 1880s. The waterwheel and most of the machinery have been retained. Now forms a reception centre for visitors to Maes Howe. Tel: 01856 761606.

P 🚌 WC ♿ 🍴 S

35. UNSTAN CHAMBERED CAIRN

About 3.5M NNE of Stromness on the A965. Orkney Ferries Ltd from Kirkwall, tel: 01856 872 044. 6 HY 283 117.

A mound covering a stone burial chamber divided by slabs into five compartments. Of Neolithic date. Access to chamber. Tel: 01856 841815.

36. WESTSIDE CHURCH, TUQUOY

On the island of Westray 3M S of Pierowall village. 5 HY 455 432.

A small and elegant 12th-century nave-and-chancel church, later the parish church, now roofless. Built by a wealthy Norse chieftain, the remains of whose farm can be seen in the adjacent cliff section. Tel: 01856 841 815.

🥾

37. WIDEFORD HILL CHAMBERED CAIRN

About 2M W of Kirkwall on the B9056. 6 HY 409 122.

A fine Neolithic chambered cairn with three concentric walls and a burial chamber with three large cells. Access to chamber. 0.5m hillwalk, which can be muddy, to property. Tel: 01856 841815.

🥾

Joint ticket for all staffed Orkney monuments. Summer: Adult £11.00 Child £3.50 Reduced £8.00. Winter: Adult £10.00 Child £3.00 Reduced £7.00.

32.

SHETLAND

7.

1. CLICKIMIN BROCH

About 1M SW of Lerwick on the A970.
4 HU 464 408.

A good example of a broch tower with associated secondary buildings of Iron Age date. Tel: 01466 793191.

2. FORT CHARLOTTE

In centre of Lerwick. 4 HU 475 415.

A five-sided artillery fort with bastions projecting from each corner. The walls are high and massive. It was built in 1665 to protect the Sound of Bressay from the Dutch, but taken by them and burned in 1673. It was rebuilt in 1781. Keys available locally during the standard opening times published in this guide. Tel: 01466 793191.

3. JARLSHOF PREHISTORIC AND NORSE SETTLEMENT

At Sumburgh Head, 22M S of Lerwick on the A970. 4 HU 399 095.

An extraordinarily important site with a complex of ancient settlements within three acres. The oldest is a Bronze Age village of oval stone huts. Above this there are an Iron Age broch and wheelhouses, and higher still an entire Viking settlement. On the crest of the mount is a house built around 1600. Visitor centre has displays on prehistoric life and history of the site. Open summer only. Tel: 01950 460112.

★★★★ Grading.
Admission: Adult £3.00 Child £1.00 Reduced £2.20.

P 🚌 🏛 Ⓢ 💷

4. MOUSA BROCH

On the island of Mousa, accessible by boat from Sandwick, about 14M S of Lerwick on the A970. For ferry contact operator, tel: 01950 431367.
4 HU 457 237.

The finest surviving Iron Age broch tower. It stands to a height of over 13.3 metres. Tel: 01466 793191.

👣

5. MUNESS CASTLE

On Island of Unst 4M NE from pier at Belmont off the A968. 1 HP 629 012.

A late 16th-century tower house with circular towers at diagonally opposite corners. The northernmost castle in the British Isles, Muness has remarkably fine architectural details. Tel: 01466 793191.

6. NESS OF BURGI

At the S-Easternmost point of Scatness, South Shetland off the A970. Access is across rocks. 4 HU 388 084.

A defensive stone-built blockhouse, probably of Iron Age date, with some features resembling a broch. Access is difficult. Tel: 01466 793191.

7. SCALLOWAY CASTLE

In Scalloway, 6M from Lerwick on the A970. 4 HU 405 393.

A fine castellated mansion built in 1600 by Patrick Stewart, Earl of Orkney, who was notorious for his cruelty. Open to the public during Shetland Woollen Company shop opening hours of 9.30am to 5.00pm, Monday to Saturday. On Sundays the key is available from the Royal Hotel. Tel: 01466 793191.

P 🖾

8. STANEYDALE 'TEMPLE'

3M SW of Bixter on West mainland off the A971. Follow marker poles, route can be very wet. 3 HU 285 502.

A Neolithic hall, heel-shaped externally, and containing a large oval chamber. Around it are ruins of houses, walls and cairns of the same period. Tel: 01466 793191.

3.

ALPHABETICAL LISTING

A

Aberdour Castle and Garden 25

Aberlemno Sculptured Stones 59

Abernethy Round Tower 55

Achnabreck Cup and Ring Marks 38

Arbroath Abbey 59

Ardchattan Priory 34

Ardclach Bell Tower 47

Ardestie Earth-House 59

Ardunie Roman Signal Station 57

Argyll's Lodging 41

Auchagallon Stone Circle 43

Auchindoun Castle 63

B

Ballygowan Cup and Ring Marks 38

Baluachraig Cup and Ring Marks 38

Balvaird Castle 55

Balvenie Castle 63

Bar Hill Fort 29

Barochan Cross 30

Barsalloch Fort 13

Bearsden Bathhouse 29

Beauly Priory 47

Biggar Gasworks Museum 30

Bishop's and Earl's Palaces, Kirkwall 69

Blackhammer Chambered Cairn 69

Blackhill Camp 57

Black House complex, Arnol 51

Blackness Castle 34

Bonawe Iron Furnace 34

Bothwell Castle 30

Brandsbutt Symbol Stone 63

Brechin Cathedral Round Tower 59

Bridge of Oich 47

Broch of Gurness (Aikerness Broch) 70

Brough of Birsay 69

Broughty Castle 60

Burghead Well 63

Burleigh Castle 55

C

Cadzow Castle 31

Caerlaverock Castle 13

Cairn Holy Chambered Cairns 13

Cairn o'Get 47

Cairnbaan Cup and Ring Marks 38

Cairnpapple Hill 19

Calanais Standing Stones & Visitor Centre 51

Cambuskenneth Abbey 34

Cardoness Castle 14

Carlungie Earth-House 60

Carn Ban 43

Carn Liath 47

Carnasserie Castle 34

Carsluith Castle 14

Castle Campbell and Garden 35

Castle of Old Wick 47

Castle Semple Collegiate Church 44

Castle Sween 35

Castlecary 33

Castlecary to Westerwood (Garnhall District) 30

Castlelaw Hill Fort 19

Caterthuns (Brown and White) 60

Chapel Finian 14

Chesters Hill Fort 19

Clackmannan Tower 35

Clava Cairns 48

Claypotts Castle 60

Click Mill, Dounby 70

Clickimin Broch 75

Cnoc Freiceadain Long Cairns 48

Corgarff Castle 63

Corrimony Chambered Cairn 48

Corstorphine Dovecot 19

Coulter Motte 31

Craigmillar Castle 19

Craignethan Castle 31

Crichton Castle 20

Crookston Castle 31

Cross Kirk, Peebles 9

Crossraguel Abbey 44
Croy Hill 29
Cubbie Row's Castle 70
and St Mary's Chapel
Cullerlie Stone Circle 64
Culross Abbey 25
Culsh Earth House 64
Cuween Hill 70
Chambered Cairn

D

Dallas Dhu Distillery 64
Deer Abbey 64
Dere Street 9
Roman Road, Soutra
Deskford Church 64
Dirleton Castle 20
and Garden
Dogton Stone 25
Doonhill Homestead 20
Doune Castle 35
Druchtag Motte 14
Drumcoltran Tower 14
Drumtroddan Cup 14
and Ring Marked Rocks
Drumtroddan 14
Standing Stones
Dryburgh Abbey 9
Duff House 64
Duffus Castle 64
Dullatur 30
Dumbarton Castle 36
Dun Beag 48
Dun Carloway 51
Dun Dornaigil 48
Dunadd Fort 39
Dunblane Cathedral 36
Dunchraigaig Cairn 39
Dundonald Castle 44
Dundrennan Abbey 15
Dunfallandy Stone 55
Dunfermline Abbey 25
and Palace
Dunglass Collegiate 20
Church

Dunkeld Cathedral 56
Dunstaffnage Castle 36
and Chapel
Dupplin Cross 20
Dwarfie Stane 70
Dyce Symbol Stones 65

E

Eagle Rock, Cramond 20
Earl's Bu and Church, 70
Orphir
Earl's Palace, Birsay 70
Eassie Sculptured Stone 60
Easter Aquhorthies 65
Stone Circle
Edin's Hall Broch 10
Edinburgh Castle 21
Edrom Church 10
Edzell Castle 60
and Garden
Eileach an Naoimh 36

Eilean Mor: 36
St Cormac's Chapel
Elcho Castle 56
Elgin Cathedral 65
Eynhallow Church 70

F

Fort Charlotte 75
Fort George 48
Fortrose Cathedral 48
Foulden Tithe Barn 10
Fowlis Wester 56
Sculptured Stone

G

Glasgow Cathedral 31
Glebe Cairn, Kilmartin 39
Glenbuchat Castle 65
Glenelg Brochs: Dun 48
Telve and Dun Troddan
Glenluce Abbey 15
Grain Earth House 71
Greenknowe Tower 10
Grey Cairns of Camster 49

H

Hackness Martello 71
Tower and Battery
Hailes Castle 21
Hermitage Castle 10
Hill o' Many Stanes 49
Hilton of Cadboll 49
Chapel
Holm of Papa Westray 71
Chambered Cairn
Holyrood Abbey 21
and Abbey Strand
Holyrood Park 21
Huntingtower Castle 56
Huntly Castle 65

I

Inchcolm Abbey 26
Inchkenneth Chapel 37
Inchmahome Priory 37
Innerpeffray Chapel 56
Inverlochy Castle 49
Iona Abbey 37
and Nunnery
Iona, MacLean's Cross 37

J

Jarlshof Prehistoric 75
and Norse Settlement
Jedburgh Abbey 10

K

Keills Chapel 38
Kelso Abbey 11
Kilberry Sculptured 38
Stones
Kilchurn Castle 38
Kildalton Cross 38
Kildrummy Castle 66
Kilmartin Sculptured 39
Stones
Kilmichael Glassary 39
Cup and Ring Marks
Kilmodan Sculptured 40
Stones
Kilmory Knap Chapel 40

Kilpatrick Dun 43
(or Cashel)
Kilwinning Abbey 45
King's Knot 41
Kinkell Church 66
Kinnaird Head Castle 66
Lighthouse
Kinneil House 40
Kirkmadrine Early 15
Christian Stones
Kisimul Castle 52
Knap of Howar 71
Knocknagael 49
Boar Stone
Knowe of Yarso 71
Chambered Cairn

L

Laggangairn Standing 15
Stones
Largs Old Kirk 45
Lauderdale Aisle, 22
St Mary's Church
Lincluden Collegiate 15
Church
Lindsay Burial Aisle 60
Links of Noltland 71
Linlithgow Palace 22
Loanhead Stone Circle 66
Loch Doon Castle 45
Lochleven Castle 56
Lochmaben Castle 15
Lochranza Castle 43

M

Machrie Moor 43
Stone Circles
MacLellan's Castle 16
Maes Howe 71
Chambered Cairn
Maiden Stone 66
Maison Dieu Chapel, 61
Brechin
Mar's Wark 41

Maybole Collegiate 45
Church
Meigle Sculptured 61
Stone Museum
Melrose Abbey 11
Memsie Cairn 66
Merkland Cross 16
Midhowe Broch 72
Midhowe Chambered 72
Cairn
Morton Castle 16
Moss Farm Road 44
Stone Circle
Mousa Broch 75
Muir o' Fauld Roman 57
Signal Station
Muness Castle 76
Muthill Old Church 57
and Tower

N

Ness of Burgi 76
Nether Largie Cairns 39
New Abbey Corn Mill 16
Newark Castle 31
Noltland Castle 72

O

Orchardton Tower 16
Ormiston Market Cross 22

P

Peel Ring of 66
Lumphanan
Picardy Symbol Stone 66
Pierowall Church 72
Preston Market Cross 22

Q

Quoyness Chambered 72
Cairn

R

Ravenscraig Castle 26
Rennibister 72
Earth-House

Restenneth Priory 61
Ri Cruin Cairn 39
Ring of Brogar Stone 72
Circle and Henge
Rispain Camp 16
Rothesay Castle 40
Rough Castle 33
Ruthven Barracks 49
Ruthwell Cross 16

S

Scalloway Castle 76
Scotstarvit Tower 27
Seabegs Wood 33
Seton Collegiate 23
Church
Skara Brae Prehistoric 73
Village
Skipness Castle and 40
Chapel
Smailholm Tower 11
Spynie Palace 67
St Andrews Castle 26
St Andrews Cathedral 27
and St Rule's Tower
St Andrews: 27
Blackfriars Chapel
St Andrews: St Mary's 27
Church, Kirkheugh
St Andrews: West Port 27
St Blane's Church, 40
Kingarth
St Bride's Church, 31
Douglas
St Bridget's Kirk, 27
Dalgety
St Clement's Church 52
St Machar's Cathedral 67
Transepts
St Magnus Church 72
St Martin's Kirk, 22
Haddington
St Mary's Chapel, 49
Crosskirk
St Mary's Chapel, 40
Rothesay
St Mary's Church, 57
Grandtully

St Mary's Kirk, Auchindoir 67

St Ninian's Cave 17

St Ninian's Chapel 17

St Orland's Stone 61

St Peter's Kirk and Parish Cross, Duffus 67

St Serf's Church, Dunning 57

St Triduana's Chapel, Restalrig Collegiate Church 22

St Vigeans Sculptured Stones 61

Staneydale 'Temple' 76

Steinacleit Cairn and Stone Circle 52

Stirling Castle 41

Stirling Old Bridge 41

Stones of Stenness Circle and Henge 73

Sueno's Stone 67

Sunnybrae Cottage 57

Sweetheart Abbey 17

T

Tantallon Castle 23

Tarves Medieval Tomb 67

Taversöe Tuick Chambered Cairn 73

Tealing Dovecot and Earth House 61

Temple Wood Stone Circles 39

Threave Castle 17

Tolquhon Castle 67

Tomnaverie Stone Circle 67

Torhouse Stone Circle 17

Tormiston Mill 73

Torphichen Preceptory 23

Torr a'Chaisteal Fort 44

Torrylin Cairn 44

Trinity House 23

Tullibardine Chapel 57

U

Unstan Chambered Cairn 73

Urquhart Castle 49

W

Wanlockhead Beam Engine 17

Watling Lodge (East and West) 33

Westquarter Dovecot 41

Westside Church, Tuquoy 73

Whithorn Priory and Museum and the Monreith Cross 17

Wideford Hill Chambered Cairn 73

Historic Scotland has a number of sites in its care that are not currently accessible to the public. They include:

Big Balcraig & Clachan Cup Mark Rocks (Dumfries & Galloway)

Castle of Park (Dumfries & Galloway)

The Grounds, Mavisbank (Edinburgh & Lothians)

Invercauld Bridge (Aberdeen & Grampian)

Kirkconnel Stones (Dumfries & Galloway)

Kirkhill Signal Station

Knock Castle (Aberdeen & Grampian)

Rowallan Castle (Ayrshire & Arran)

St Serf's Priory, Loch Leven (Perthshire)

Stanley Mills, Stanley (Perthshire)

The Wren's Egg Stone Circle (Dumfries & Galloway)

HISTORIC SCOTLAND